CRICKET IN WALES

The History of Blaina Cricket Club

Little Club – Big Story

ANDREW HIGNELL

St David's Press
Cardiff

Published in Wales by St. David's Press, an imprint of
Ashley Drake Publishing Ltd
PO Box 733
Cardiff
CF14 2ZY
www.st-davids-press.com

First Impression – 2012

ISBN 978-1-902719-32-0

© Ashley Drake Publishing Ltd 2012
Text © Andrew Hignell 2012

The right of Andrew Hignell to be identified as the author of this work has been asserted in accordance with the Copyright Design and Patents Act of 1988.

All rights reserved. No part of this publication may be reproduced, stored in a retrieval system, or transmitted, in any form or by any means without the prior permission of the publishers.

British Library Cataloguing-in-Publication Data.
A CIP catalogue for this book is available from the British Library.

Typeset by White Lotus Infotech Pvt. Ltd, Puducherry, India.
Printed by MPG Books Group Ltd, Bodmin, Cornwall.

CONTENTS

Dedication	v
List of Subscribers	vi
Foreword	vii
Acknowledgements	ix
Introduction	xi
1. Levick's Legacy	1
2. The Second Club	14
3. The Rise of Monmouthshire and the Creation of Central Park	22
4. The Arrival of Evan Watkins	33
5. Joining the South Wales Cricket Association	39
6. The First Golden Era	47
7. The Bubble Bursts	59
8. Bodyline at Blaina!	66
9. The Cricketers Go to War	73
10. Leagues and Championships	79
11. International Cricket Comes to Blaina	84
12. Cricket on Sundays	91
13. Overcoming the Difficulties of the 1960s	98
14. Rebuilding in the 1970s	106
15. A Return to the Premier Division	115
16. The Resurrection of Tours	123
17. The Joy of Six!	131
18. Promotion and Relegation	139
19. Blaina CC Enters the Twenty-First Century	148
20. Blaina Cricket Club in 2011	156

Contents

Appendices 161
  A. Captains of Blaina CC: 1889–2011 161
  B. First Date of Matches Played by Cricket Clubs in the Blaina & Nantyglo Area 164
  C. Century Makers for Blaina CC 165
  D. Life Members of Blaina CC 166
  E. Chairmen of Blaina CC 166
  F. Secretaries of Blaina CC 167
  G. Treasurers of Blaina CC 168
  H. Presidents of Blaina CC 169
  I. Patrons of Blaina CC 169

This book is broadly dedicated to all of the cricketers who have represented Blaina since the club first took the field in the 19th century.

However, there is one person without whom the club might have folded. Indeed, without the efforts and influence of people such as Evan Watkins, the club of the 21st century would not be in the healthy position which it currently enjoys.

LIST OF SUBSCRIBERS

Adams, F. W.
Amos, Michael
Anstee, John
Arnold, John
Barber, Alun
Barber, Albert Ernest
Barnes, David
Barnes, Peter
Bayton, Glyn
Bevan, Simon
Brookes, Alan (Blaina CC) 1944–2010
Brookes, Gwyn & Shirley
Brookes, Maldwyn
Brookes, Paul, Sarah, Georgia & Eden
Clarke, Colin
Clarke, Michael
Cobourne, Nathan Owen
Cole, Lilian & Tony
Cook, Robert
Cooper, Alan
Cooper, Clive
Crandon, Liam
Dally, Malcolm B.
Davies, D. John
Davies, Darryl
Davies, F. A. (Jeffreys)
Davies, Glyn
Davies, Roy
Despres, Christopher
Edmunds, Ralph
Edwards, Anthony
Edwards, Douglas
Edwards, John
Edwards, Norman
Evans, David
Evans, Graham
Flight, Molly
Gillard, Peter
Gillingham, Gareth
Gomery, David
Gore, Lyndon & Suzanne
Gore, Mel & Beryl
Griffin, Graham
Griffiths, Granville
Griffiths, Howard
Haines, Phil
Hancock, Allen
Harvey, Roger
Hewitt, Julian
Holmes, Ioan
Howells, Mike
Hughes, Allen
Hughes, Graham
Hurle, Len
James, Gareth
Jefferies, Allan, Julie & Benjamin
Jeffreys, Haydn
John, Nigel
Jones, Arron
Jones, Brian & Andrew
Jones, David
Jones, Graham
Jones, Peter
Khan, Jimmy
Knight, Howard
Lewis, Alun
Lewis, Barry
Lewis, Ken
Llewelyn, Norman
Maidment, Chris
Maidment, Errol
Mogford, Roy

LIST OF SUBSCRIBERS

Morden, Alan
Morgan, David J. (George)
Morgan, Ivor G.
Morris, Rita
Nash, Wayne
Nicklin, Gary
O'Brien, Bob
O'Sullivan, A. G.
O'Sullinvan, M. A.
Olding, Frank
Pagett, Gareth
Palmer, Andrew
Palmer, Kenneth
Parkin, Pat
Pearce, Michael
Phippen, John
Pope, David G.
Pope, Neville
Pope, Roy
Powell, Dev
Pratten, John
Price, Jeff
Price, Redvers
Regan, Chris
Reynolds, David
Roberts, Allyson
Roberts, G. E. (Jeffreys)
Rowlands, Graham
Samuel, Josh

Saunders, Gareth
Seabrook, Graham
Selway, James
Silk, Linda
Silk, Graham
Sims, Eunice (Jeffreys)
Sims, Lindsay
Smith, Eric
Smith, Robert
Street, Malcolm
Sutton, Chris
Thomas, Ann
Tucker, Derry
Walding, John
Werrett, Malcolm
Williams, Alan & Diane
Williams, Andrew & Sally
Williams, Bernard
Williams, Evan Dafydd
Williams, Gareth & Angela
Williams, Maddison Summer
Williams, Maureen
Williams, Mostyn
Williams, Nic
Williams, Paul
Williams, Steve (Wig)
Witherall, Martin
Wright, John Henry

FOREWORD

Blaina is situated at the head of the Ebbw Fach valley. Bounded to the west and east by steep hills rising to over 1,500 feet, it is a far cry from the rolling downland and gentle chalk vales of south-eastern England which cricket historians regard as the cradle of the game of cricket in the seventeenth and eighteenth centuries. Yet it is at Blaina, amidst the smoke and noise from the area's ironworks that during the middle of the nineteenth century that cricket playing took place from the middle of the nineteenth century onwards, with the games having an important influence on the area's social history as well as more generally, on the development of sport and other ball games in Monmouthshire.

The history of the Blaina area is closely interwoven with the growth, and subsequent decline, of the area's iron and coal industry. The black gold and "king coal" brought fame and fortune to the area's entrepreneurs from the early 1800s onwards, whilst the influx of people to work in these heavy industries also brought skills, knowledge and new ideas to the area, not least in terms of healthy recreation and lifestyles.

However, the industrial boom of the early 19th century was not without its problems, especially the grim and desperate living conditions of the workers, many of whom were virtual slaves to the ironmasters and colliery owners working long hours, in dark and dirty conditions for, quite often, modest wages. The seeds of industrial unrest and Chartism were sown in the Blaina area, especially a few miles to the north at Nantyglo. Yet it was against this background of fractured relations between the rich and the working classes that cricket began in the 1850s as the ironmasters used the game to fly the flag for their works as well as trying to harmonise industrial relations and promoting healthy lifestyles.

The playing of cricket subsequently developed into a unifying force within the tight-knit valley communities and, as the first team-game to evolve in industrial Wales, it helped to bond and give immense pleasure to the people whose livelihoods were dominated by the state of the iron and coal industries.

There were good times and bad, yet throughout the nineteenth and twentieth centuries the Blaina cricket club remained strong and vibrant. For example, it was a founding member of the South Wales and Monmouthshire Leagues, created in 1926 as the leading cricket clubs from the south-east and west of Wales came together, with Blaina's games watched by crowds of up to 4,000. Unlike other clubs in the region, it has successfully ridden out the grim

FOREWORD

The Blaina band

years when the iron trade slumped or the output of coal fell. Indeed, some of the club's strongest years, measured by on-field performances and results, have come during trade depressions.

This book recalls these Golden Years in the history of Blaina CC as well as tracing the fascinating history of cricket in this Monmouthshire valley from the times when coal was king, through the years of the decline in the iron and tinplate industry to the modern years of mine closure and deindustrialisation, drawing on the memories and personal recollections of those directly involved with the Blaina club.

ACKNOWLEDGEMENTS

A book of this nature would not have been possible without the support of the Blaina Club. I have been most fortunate to have been able to call upon the methodical research work of Alan and Diane Williams, as well as the club records of Darryl Davies. Alan, Diane and Darryl formed a superb research team who were prepared to seek out many nuggets which lay in the dark and remote recesses of local newspapers. Their tireless and painstaking research has formed the foundation for the research which went into this book and without their diligence and enthusiasm, I would have floundered in a sea of uncertainty.

The gleeful enthusiasm of Emma Peplow, and the eager assistance of her colleagues at the MCC Library at Lord's, all helped to transform what started out as a dream of finding out about the history of the club, and a pilot project with the *Taking the Field Project*, into the reality of this handsome book. The subsequent support of Professors Mike Wilson and Hamish Fyfe, plus the guiding hands of Adam Chadwick and Neil Robinson at the MCC, also enabled smooth progress with the *Taking the Field Project* and provided a fund of anecdotes and recollections upon which further newspaper research could be undertaken.

Club stalwarts Alun Lewis and Dai Cobourne each helped to add extra information, whilst the lucid reminiscences of Ernie Barber, Mel Gore, Alun Barber, Chris Despres, David Gomery, Alan Cooper, Andrew Palmer and Liam Crandon, plus the assistance of Mrs Meyrick at the Blaina Heritage Centre, all proved invaluable information for which I am most grateful.

Last, but by no means least, my thanks to Ashley Drake at the St. David's Press for his support of my research and producing this fine volume which will stand as a fitting testament to the many men and women who have ensured that Blaina CC has survived into the 21st century.

Andrew Hignell
Cardiff, March 2012

INTRODUCTION

"Beginnings" are sometimes tricky to pin down. Even if we are taught from school that every story should have a beginning, middle and end, life does not always work out quite as neatly as we would like it to. Luckily for me, having been asked to write this introduction to the history of Blaina Cricket Club, the beginning of the club's journey to discover its past is clear, and one that everyone involved remembers. It was, in fact, the first story the Blaina members told me when we first met in October 2010.

In the mid-2000s, Darryl Davies, committee member and long-standing opening bowler, was enjoying a family day out in Bryn Bach Park, Tredegar. Having wandered over to the cafe for an ice cream, Darryl noticed a photograph on the wall. The photo was of a game of cricket in the 1920s, with thousands of people sat watching in the sunshine. The setting seemed uncannily familiar to Darryl, who later told me:

> I went to have a look at it and I saw straight away that it was Blaina – because of the green shed where the players used to change from. There was no writing above it, it just said "A Cricket Match". I thought this was a great photograph because of the thousands of people sat down on the ground watching the cricket, they all had flat caps on so I guessed it'd be the 1920s era, and I thought it would be a great photograph for us to have.

When Darryl returned to Blaina he told long-time players, committee-men and stalwarts of Blaina CC Alan Williams and Alun Lewis about the photograph. Unfortunately for the club, although useful for an enigmatic opening story, the photograph disappeared before the club could get a copy of it.

Despite this, the photograph sparked the interest of several members of the club. There had been some talk about researching Blaina CC's history for many years, but until now these stirrings had not been followed up. The members and committee knew little about the club's past, and worst of all, no-one in the club could shed any light on what the game in the photograph was, or why so many people would be watching a match on Central Park. It was a few months later that Alan Williams, on his annual holiday to Oxwich Bay, noticed the same photograph in the Swansea Maritime Museum. Again, the infamous "green shed" meant that he was certain the photograph was of Central Park.

The club now finally had a copy of this photograph, but not the answers to their questions. The clubs records only went back to the 1960s, and the

INTRODUCTION

A packed Central Park in 1926 for a game in the South Wales and Monmouthshire League

1920s were too long ago for most of the old Blaina players to remember! Alan Williams decided to approach Glamorgan County Cricket Club's archivist and scorer Andrew Hignell for his advice on how to start researching and preserving their history. Directed to newspapers that they had never heard of, held in the nearby Newport Archives, a group of historians emerged to record Blaina CC's past: first of all Darryl Davies and Alan Williams, later joined by Alan's wife Diane, David Cobourne and Alun Lewis.

Starting in the mid-1920s, the club historians discovered that their club had a bigger history than they had ever imagined. As Darryl later told me:

> When we found that they were indeed a huge side, a great side – one of the top sides in Wales, so we...well, we were a bit shocked really.

Over the next two years these historians started to piece together the history of Blaina Cricket Club; the story that will be told in the following pages. This group spent many hours not only reading the archive but collecting photographs and artefacts and, thanks largely to Diane, cataloguing the information they gathered. There were many surprises along the way: just how old

INTRODUCTION

the club was, and how much cricket was played around Blaina before the Second World War. There were great characters and people of distinction, as well as hard times for club members and supporters, dependent as they were on the turbulent mines and local industry for their livelihoods. Throughout all, Blaina Cricket Club survived, thrived, and became a vital part of the lives of many local people.

I first met these historians in October 2010, eighteen months into their research and two months into my new job at the Marylebone Cricket Club (MCC). I was employed as Research Associate on a joint grassroots cricket history project with the University of Glamorgan called "Taking the Field" (TTF). TTF was set-up to help collect and share the stories and histories of grassroots cricket clubs in the UK and Sri Lanka using oral history interviews, collecting photographs and creating "digital stories" – short oral histories complemented with music, video and photographs. The project emerged from a former University of Glamorgan project called "TaleEnders" which charted the history of several Welsh grassroots clubs in this way; TTF was established to expand the idea into England and beyond. It was therefore fitting that TTF's first club was Blaina, still in the Welsh valleys.

TTF celebrates the histories of grassroots cricket clubs through our website – www.takingthefield.com – and exhibitions in the MCC Museum at Lord's. We've worked directly with clubs all across the country, but we also encourage any grassroots club to sign up to our website and start recording their own history, begin oral history interviews and create digital stories. All the guides needed to start this process are available online and we hope that in the future we'll hear the stories from many UK clubs. At TTF we want to go beyond the cricket, to hear about the history of the club and all involved – the young players, the old stalwarts, the tea ladies – and how they have interacted with their local community over the years. It was partly for this reason that Andrew Hignell decided to introduce me to Blaina CC.

Before my first meeting with the Blaina historians I remember nervously putting together a presentation to explain what we wanted to do at TTF. I did not even get halfway through it, however, before the Blaina members' enthusiasm and interest spilled over and a discussion about the possibilities took over! They were so full of ideas and suggestions for stories, quickly showing me their collection of photographs and all the research they had done to date, that I knew that working with them would be a fantastic success. A few weeks later I was visiting Blaina for the first time and being welcomed into Alan and Diane Williams' home, the stories were already flowing and we had lots of ideas for interview topics, questions and the final stories that the club wanted to emerge from their collaboration with TTF.

INTRODUCTION

With club members and Andrew researching hard in the archives to piece together the fantastic story told in this book, my role with TTF was to conduct oral history interviews and bring out the anecdotes and details that scorebooks, club committee minutes and newspaper reports do not always record. There certainly was no shortage of these from our interviews. On two extremely busy days in a cold November, I interviewed 13 local people involved with the club, from lifelong supporter Ernie Barber, who was still going strong in his 80s, to 17 year old Liam Crandon, one of the current first team stars, and asked about all sorts of memories from the club: how they became involved, what they enjoyed most, their favourite matches, the tours and the social life. The answers I got were fantastic.

Stories and anecdotes emerged from throughout the years. Ernie Barber, for example, told me about his childhood summers that revolved around watching the great 1920s Blaina team play. To get to matches Ernie would have to sneak through the local colliery, Beynon's, and when doing so he was not always able to avoid the company sergeant Davis and his dog! Ten year-old Ernie had not quite finished causing trouble, as he and his friends would slip into Central Park without paying the entrance fee and sit on the bank just outside. The boys would always stay out late to watch the second innings, upsetting their mothers and missing their tea, instead sharing one packet of peanuts between them all. Ernie shared fond memories of his boyhood friends and spoke about the success of the club with great pride.

Later stories from the 1980s revealed the social side and friendships that emerged within Blaina CC. Darryl Davies remembered the team heading to Abergavenny to watch a Glamorgan CCC match. Knowing the local players, the Blaina team were able to watch from the players' bar, and after the match ended up drinking with one I. T. Botham, who to the team's delight had heard of the great wicket at Central Park. At the same time, a journalist from the local paper was waiting for Viv Richards to emerge from the dressing room and comment on the match. By this time some of the Blaina CC lads had consumed a few pints, and one of them decided the journalist had waited long enough. Bursting into the dressing room armed with the back of a receipt and a bookie's pencil, he cried out: "I'm from the local paper, Mr Richards. Any thoughts on the match?" Needless to say the West Indian star declined this impromptu offer and the Blaina player was quickly shown the dressing room door.

From a different viewpoint, Diane Williams, tea lady for many years, remembers a particular day in 1981: the wedding of Charles and Diana. The extra Bank Holiday to celebrate the wedding shows the different priorities of the men and women of Blaina:

INTRODUCTION

Unknown to me the boys went and made a fixture... I wanted to sit in front of the TV. The only course left was to put a trestle-table up in my front room so I could make the food in there and still watch the wedding. The boys were then left to fend for themselves.

Seeing as the match was arranged without consulting their all important tea lady this can only have served the boys right!

As an outsider coming in to Blaina, I was impressed by a number of things about the club and its members. Firstly, it was overwhelmingly clear how important the club was to everyone and how much pride they had in it and their community. This was put beautifully by Alun Lewis:

The club has been bound together by a tremendous spirit and camaraderie by everybody...I'm not saying that we're unique in Blaina, we're not. But we're in a part of the world that isn't conducive to good weather, that isn't conducive to playing all summer...but we've always kept together. As I say, we've had financial troubles, we've had bare times, but it's always been there – we've always found a raft of people whose only interest in the cricket club is to keep it going – and they've always done that.

This spirit will emerge clearly in the pages of this book. In particular, the two major periods of success for the club, the 1920s and the 1980s, were during some really tough economic times for the local area. The success of Blaina in the South Wales and Monmouthshire League in the 1920s was matched by three promotions for the first team in four or five years during the 1980s. In this period the club introduced a large number of young, extremely talented players into the side; Central Park was brought back to its usual high standard, and the old "green shack" pavilion – which by that point "felt like it had been erected in the times of Crawshay Bailey" according to Blaina player Chris Despres – was finally replaced. Chris remembers this 1980s team fondly:

I really enjoyed the standard of cricket we were playing, but particularly the camaraderie of the team. We were going places, there was only one way we were going: up the leagues and we were playing some seriously good cricket. It was a delight to go out and compete at that level.

Challenges continue to present themselves to the team today, from disasters with the pavilion to having to travel all over Wales just to play in the new league set-up, but Blaina is certainly a club and a community that will not go down without a fight.

Secondly, the club has always played an important part in local life, in particular the long tradition of encouraging boys to learn and play cricket. Ernie Barber remembers the star players helping the boys of the town with their batting and bowling during summer evenings in the 1920s, and through

INTRODUCTION

the 1970s and 1980s local schoolteachers David Gomery and Chris Despres ensured that the most talented pupils were brought into the club and trained in the second team. Chris is still fulfilling this role now, whilst others such as Darryl Davies and Alan Williams look for ways they can offer the current boys more, and more professional, training. In this way the next batch of Blaina teenagers will learn to play and love the game of cricket, something vital for the community. As David Gomery told me: "it's something to help keep the boys off the streets," and long may it continue.

There are other ways that the club managed to help out the town as a whole. After they were promoted to the Glamorgan and Gwent Premier League in 1982, the club members decided to mark the occasion by planting a row of Leylandii trees along the edge of Central Park. This was for more than aesthetic reasons, as Central Park is on former spoil-tip ground. After the disaster in Aberfan these sites were being treated in a completely different way, and Alan Williams, who was groundsman at the time, felt that the club ought to do their bit. Alan ensured that the money was raised and planted the trees himself, which have become, in his words, a "bit of a landmark" in the town.

> It's something that the people in the cricket club know about, something that we did for the community...it's only a small thing but instead of wasting our money having a good drink to celebrate we thought we'd plant the trees, and we're very pleased with our legacy.

I imagine that the Blaina boys did indeed have a reasonably good drink to celebrate their promotion, but the trees themselves are a lasting and welcome addition to Central Park. Alan spoke with great pride of his time as groundsman: "It was an honour to look after the ground." His efforts were certainly well appreciated by every other club member I spoke to about that time. The strength of feeling for Blaina's beautiful ground (and its fantastic pitch) came through loud and clear. As current Chairman Andrew Palmer told me:

> If I had the last days of my life...I would be up on that park – it's where I'd want to be...it's a wonderful place to play cricket, in the summer when the sun is shining...it's absolutely beautiful. You won't beat Blaina, not on Central Park.

Finally, throughout the years the club has worked hard to keep playing cricket and to make sure that the costs of the ground are affordable for all to join in. Despite cricket sometimes having a reputation for snobbery or elitism, there's none of this in the atmosphere around Central Park. Blaina members told me proudly how they have managed to keep match fees and club subscriptions as low as possible to make sure everyone has a chance to play. Money was raised through bar receipts, raffles, car boot sales and even some more outlandish schemes, such as a bed push to Nevill Hall hospital in Abergavenny

INTRODUCTION

Central Park, as seen from the pavilion

and a parachute jump by David Morgan! These efforts ensure that anyone, irrespective of their economic circumstances, can play cricket with the club.

How this was organised has changed over the years however, as Mel Gore, who started playing for Blaina after the Second World War, told me. He was reluctant at first to be picked for the 1st XI as the side was made up of more "upper class" players, who did not enjoy the same social life that the miners and factory workers in the 2nd XI did! These divisions were soon broken down, however, and if many of the stories are anything to go by, the second XI social traditions were the ones that survive. The current club patron and former player David Jones told me during his time at the club he was introduced to all sorts of people:

> We were all local people, people that I knew but from different backgrounds completely. Some were schoolteachers, some were factory workers, some were miners – it was a good mix. You learn a lot from these blokes, apart from enjoying the game of cricket you learn so much from talking to them about their own lives, and that's enriched my life a lot.

INTRODUCTION

There were so many fantastic stories that emerged from my interviews in Blaina: tense matches, great social nights, hints of what the lads got up to on tour, visits from Glamorgan CCC, family trips to Barry, the list goes on. For TTF, this was perfect, and in late 2010 the first digital stories from Blaina started to appear online, first on Facebook and later on their own page on the TTF website. For the Middlesex-Glamorgan game at Lord's in June 2011 a special slideshow starring Blaina was in place at the MCC Museum, and was even advertised on the big screens around the ground and mentioned on the BBC Radio Wales commentary. One of my favourite TTF memories was welcoming a coachload of Blaina members to Lord's for a free tour and to see their slideshow in the MCC Museum's film theatre. An unusual way for a club to make it to the home of cricket perhaps, but one I hope they all enjoyed. The club were also presented with a special DVD of all the TTF materials.

More brushes with fame for Blaina were to come, however, during the England-Sri Lanka Test Match at the SWALEC Stadium in June 2011. I came home to Cardiff to watch the match with my Dad, Alan Williams and Darryl Davies; luckily enough on the one day that the weather held off for a full day's play. We were not just there to enjoy the cricket, but for a very special lunchtime invitation to be interviewed on Test Match Special. The TMS producers gladly invited some Welsh cricketers into the commentary box, to "hear those accents that don't normally feature on TMS"! We did not disappoint during our lunchtime slot, with a warm welcome from Aggers and a chance to share some of the history of Blaina Cricket Club on one of the most prestigious cricket broadcasts. I received emails afterwards from all over the world, including the US and several parts of Europe. The fame of Blaina has spread far and wide, thanks to the efforts of Andrew Hignell and that group of historians, first inspired by a mysterious 1920s photograph.

After finishing work with Blaina, TTF continues to collaborate with grassroots clubs from around the UK and is even researching club cricket in Sri Lanka. Even after meeting and working with new clubs involved, and hearing their stories, I'm still so pleased that Blaina were our first club. Their enthusiasm, warm hospitality – especially from Alan and Diane Williams – and fantastic history have made them the ideal club; setting a very high standard that all future clubs are measured against. I'm delighted they have achieved their aim and published this fantastic history so that the story of Blaina Cricket Club can be shared in its entirety for everyone. It is due to the hard work of that group of historians and Andrew Hignell. I'm extremely proud to have been involved at all, and especially to have been asked to contribute with this introduction.

INTRODUCTION

Back in November 2010, as Darryl Davies told me about the club's search for their history, he ended his comments with the following:

> We decided then that they [the 1920s side] were such a good side that they shouldn't be forgotten and that we'd take a lot of time and effort to research it more, which we've done...the chance of just seeing that photograph really has proved worthwhile...We seem to be on the right road and hopefully we'll put the club back on the map again.

Now that the research is done, the stories all shared and recorded in the following pages for you and future generations to enjoy, Blaina CC is certainly firmly back on the cricket world's map. It's a wonderful story of a club with a truly big history, and I hope you're as captivated by it as I was. It only remains for me to say that I'm sure you'll enjoy this fantastic book – and here's to the next 160 years!

Emma Peplow
March 2012

1
LEVICK'S LEGACY

Frederick Levick – the owner of Blaina Ironworks – was an entrepreneur with great energy and vision. Through his efforts, the Blaina works became one of the major industrial centres in northern Monmouthshire, rivalling the already well-established centres at Tredegar, Ebbw Vale and Blaenavon.

Indeed, it was Levick who was responsible for cricket being first played in the town, with a team playing Ebbw Vale in early June 1853. Like many things in mid-Victorian Blaina, the cricket club bore the stamp of the town's ironmaster as he strove to improve the living conditions of his workers, and the status of his works. A far cry from twenty years or so before a few miles to the north in Nantyglo, when fractured relations between the masters and their men led to the birth of Chartism and industrial unrest on a regional scale.

Industry had already completely changed both the way of life and the geography of the Monmouthshire valleys. Until the mid-18th century, the area around Blaina was no different to the rest of the valley, with wooded slopes – dominated by beech, oak and ash – and a series of scattered farms where the owners grew corn and oats, besides keeping a few cattle and sheep. There were only a hundred or so dwellings in the entire parish, and overall there was a very gentle pace to life. If any recreation took place, it was probably when the locals visited the fairs at Abergavenny.

The pastoral landscape started to change in the late 18th century as industrial activity began, with some small-scale coal mining plus the digging of ironstone and iron ore. The scale of activity increased in the closing years of the 1700s as demand for manufactured iron goods dramatically rose as a result of the Napoleonic War. The early industrialists found the local topography perfect for the extraction and smelting of the iron ore, found in abundant quantities in seams with coal and limestone, and close to fast-flowing rivers which could turn the bellows to give the necessary blast in the early furnaces.

Industrialisation began to the north at Nantyglo in the 1790s as two furnaces, several forges, a steam engine and several outbuildings were established by Harford, Hill and Company. In 1811 these were bought by Joseph Bailey and Matthew Wayne for £8,000, with Joseph's brother Crawshay,

Blaina ironworks

joining him in 1820 and overseeing a phase of expansion as the pace of industrialisation quickened. By 1825 there were seven furnaces at Nantyglo, with over 500 houses where the workers lived.

The Blaina ironworks were founded in 1823 by George Jones, an ironmaster and capitalist from Staffordshire, and John Barker, another entrepreneur from the Wolverhampton area. The owners exploited the small furnaces to their limit, producing around 2,400 tons of iron per annum, before selling the works to Thomas Brown and John Russell from Pontymister. With demand for iron continuing to rise, the 1840s witnessed a dramatic increase in industrial activity at Blaina as the works became the property of Brown and his new partner Frederick Levick, who had moved to the ironworks to be deputy manager.

Annual output from the Blaina works soon topped 5,200 tonnes, and with demand continuing to exceed supply, Levick and Brown spent over half a million pounds purchasing some of the smaller freehold works in the area, as well as in 1855, the well-established Coal Brook Vale works which had been in operation since 1820.

A general view of Blaina in the early 20th century

The rapid industrialisation though had its costs, especially with the workers housing. No thought was given to the effectiveness of the accommodation which was erected quickly and in many cases with little attention to basic services and sanitation. Despite the success of the ironmasters, overcrowding and illness were commonplace and settlements such as Nantyglo and Blaina were riddled with inadequate housing and the threat of disease.

These two towns in the Monmouthshire valleys also earned a certain notoriety by being one of the earliest centres of the Chartist uprising during the 1830s and early 1840s. This was a working-class rebellion against the ruling upper classes, although the seeds for labour unrest were sown much earlier in the 19th century. After the Napoleonic Wars, the price of iron fell from £20 per ton to £8 and this dramatic drop affected the wages of the workers, which also sharply fluctuated. In a bid to lower their production costs, the ironmasters tried to reduce the workers wages, but this produced a dramatic response in 1816 as workers in Nantyglo protested, fearful that their livelihoods would deteriorate even further.

Whilst the ironmasters, such as the Baileys of Nantyglo House, lived in grand mansions, reflecting their burgeoning wealth and apparent power

The remains of the Nantyglo Roundhouses

within the local community, the majority of workers lived in squalid and insanitary conditions, working long shifts for little monetary reward and, during the winter months, seeing precious little daylight.

As a result of these Spartan conditions, labour unrest and militancy became commonplace and in February 1822 the workers at the Blaina works went on strike to protest at a proposed 6% cut in their wages. A few black-legs continued to work, but on the night of February 17th, 1822 an attempt at retribution was rather violently handed out as a gang of between 150 and 200 men – all with blackened faces – descended on the homes of two of the black-legs. Windows were smashed, the doors were forced open, their furniture was smashed up and the two men were beaten up. In April a gang of men also travelled over the hillsides to Abersychan and destroyed the house of a black-leg who had worked in Nantyglo.

A group of Nantyglo workers also defeated local militiamen and reinforcements were summoned to restore order, with a detachment from the Scots

Greys being billeted locally for several weeks. In fact, the situation was so grave that Lord Melbourne, the Home Secretary, visited Abergavenny to discuss the situation with local magistrates, whilst Crawshay Bailey so feared for his life that he built two fortified towers – the Nantyglo Roundhouses – for his own protection. After several months, some of the leaders of the gang were discovered, tried and executed, but the events were the forerunner of the Miners Federation, and by 1830 the Friendly Society of Coal Mining had union clubs in both Nantyglo and Blaina.

More organised protests duly came during the Chartist Movement during the 1830s with Nantyglo being the home of Zephaniah Williams, a local collier and innkeeper, who was one of the local leaders of the Movement and, on November 3rd, 1839, he led a column of men from Nantyglo to Newport. Their protest became bloody as the following morning they stormed the Westgate Hotel. But a group of soldiers were waiting inside, and a volley of shots were fired during which 22 people were killed and a further 50 injured. Williams and several other leaders of the Movement were arrested, tried and found guilty. The original death sentence though was commuted to transportation, with Williams being shipped to a penal colony in Australia. He was eventually pardoned in 1854, by which time he had settled with his wife in Tasmania, where he subsequently discovered coal and made a considerable fortune after founding the Tasmanian coal trade.

By the time Williams was pardoned, cricket had been played in his home town, with the first match on record being a game in August 1851 at Tredegar. The playing of cricket was part of an attempt to generate more harmonious relationships between the ironmasters and their staff. The fact that this initial game, like the subsequent fixture in July 1852 against Dowlais, was against a team from a neighbouring iron-making centre also hints at a novel form of harnessing the inter-valley rivalry and the competitiveness between the iron-making companies.

With such a long history of workers' unrest and trade union activity, it was no coincidence that Frederick Levick was eager to be seen as a kindly employer and, in 1853, he organised a match between his Blaina works and their counterparts from Ebbw Vale. Born in London in 1804, Levick was a very capable entrepreneur with good business skills, having learnt the iron trade in the Black Country and working with various companies in the Wolverhampton area. In 1839 he moved to South Wales to work as the deputy manager of the Blaina, Cwm Celyn and Coalbrookvale ironworks, and in 1844 he became the Works manager, before purchasing the works with John Simpson in 1846.

During his years of management, the Ironworks increased their activity with Levick using his entrepreneurial skills to diversify his business portfolio. For example, in 1854 he became a Director (along with Abraham Darby,

Thomas Brown, William Tothill and Joseph Robinson) of the West Somerset Mineral Railway which ran from Watchet on the Severn coast inland to Brompton Regis. Opened in 1856, the line allowed iron ore and limestone to be brought from the West Country to South Wales and provided the Blaina works with a new outlet for their products as well as allowing the raw materials to be transported across the Severn. In 1855 Levick also became a partner in the Brendon Hills Iron Ore Company, before developing some business interests at Shirenewton in Gloucestershire. Flushed with this success, in 1858 he was able to buy out the other partners at the Blaina Works and became the sole owner of the six furnaces.

In records from 1859 he is listed as a resident of Wain Wern House near Pontypool and, besides being a successful businessman, Levick was a happy family man, having married Alice Parry Gabb with whom he had seven children – Frederick Carlton, George David, Thomas Carlton, William Parry, Ethel Mary, Rose Helena, and Jane Elizabeth who in 1860 married J Hawker Soper, the surgeon at the Blaina Works.

Levick had a strong social conscience, and was appalled at the lifestyles of some of his men as shown by his comments in 1854 when called to give evidence to the Westminster government's Payment of Wages committee – "the extent to which men go to the public houses is one of my greatest troubles in managing the works and I would take any other possible means to prevent them." Indeed, there were many pubs in Blaina with Slaters Directory for 1852/53 listing eight establishments – The Blaina Inn, Castle, Crown, Globe, Lion, The Rolling Mill, The White Lion and The Yew Tree – before Morris' Directory for 1862 added a further six – Lamb Inn, The Rising Sun, Colliers Arms, Red Lion, Ballers Arms and The Griffin.

The public houses though were also the place where some of the workers received their wages, so after all of their manual labour in hot and sweaty conditions, it was no surprise that the workers would quickly spend some of their hard-earned cash on a quick libation or two. The problem of drunkenness was also commented upon by various official reports – for example the Commission of Inquiry into the State of Education in Wales in 1847 commented how the area "contains a larger proportion of dissolute people of both sexes than almost any other populace…." whilst Birch (1959) refers to another report from the mid-19th century which stated how "one effect of the severe heat and exertion is the creation of a craving for stimulants, such as beer, which at once cool and support the workmen, and to a certain extent no-one would grudge them these, but unfortunately, the craving does not always cease with the work." *(quoted in Alan Birch, The Economic history of the British iron and steel industry 1784–1879, Frank Cass, London, 1959)*

Living conditions were also grim, with a government report finding in Nantyglo and Blaina that "overcrowded houses and the dirt and discomfort around them contributed to destroy the decencies of domestic life and to drive the old and young to the beer houses which offered them temptation at every step." *(1874 – Report of the Commission on Education in Wales)*

Similarly, a report by the Inspector of Nuisances on the sanitary conditions in Blaina found near the centre of the town "an open gutter or cesspool which is quite stagnant and a receptacle for all soap suds and other filth from the whole of the area." (Report by the Inspector of Nuisances in June 1861) A further report found about 600 dwellings in Blaina to be lacking the basic sanitary accommodation (report in May 1862).

Levick took steps to try and improve conditions, donating £4,000 in 1857 towards the construction of a new church, whilst he also agreed to act as the President of the Blaina Instruction Society. It was no surprise that Levick saw the encouragement of playing cricket as another, albeit small, step forward in further improving the lifestyles of his men, as well as helping to forge harmonious relations between his staff and promoting the good name of his Ironworks.

The initial matches took place in May and June 1853 against Ebbw Vale and Tredegar on Duffryn Field – the site where a dozen or so years later, the town's gasworks was built. In September, a further fixture followed as the Blaina team met the young gentlemen of the St.Woollo's club from Newport. Fixtures remained sporadic for the next few years; in 1856 a match was staged against Tredegar, followed in 1857 by a game with Pontypool. The Blaina club met other iron-making centres, with contests taking place on Saturday afternoons as the staff of the ironworks enjoyed their spare time in a fruitful manner – something that Levick felt strongly about given the fact that on October 1st, 1863 as a local JP he fined John Howell of Mynyddislwyn, near Blackwood, the sum of £1 for employing four young persons after 2pm on Saturdays.

Memorable Matches by Darryl Davies

Number 1 – Blaina's First-ever Game

Blaina's first game took place in 1853 – it was also the first sporting occasion in the area between two representative teams. The match took place at Duffryn Field on a beautiful sunny day – the contest commenced at twelve noon in front of a large assembly of spectators, including all of the local gentry and businessmen, with entertainment provided by the Blaina Brass Band, whilst the catering and refreshments were supplied by a Mr Igglesden.

THE HISTORY OF BLAINA CRICKET CLUB

The game had been set up as a two innings per side affair, with the highest aggregate determining the victors. Some large bets had been placed on the Blaina side.

Ebbw Vale secured a two-run lead on first innings before Blaina amassed 133 in their second innings thanks to a magnificent knock of 75 by John Jones. A measure of the importance of his efforts was that no other Blaina batsman got into double figures, and it was not until the early 1900s that other batsmen surpassed his score.

Hinton then took four wickets as Blaina won by 81-runs and left the field to the delight of the crowd. Before the celebrations were over, the Blaina club also accepted the challenge of a re-match at Ebbw Vale.

Blaina

	First innings		Second innings	
J Hinton	ct Chippendale	1	lbw b Roden	8
C Widdowson	b Roden	2	lbw b Roden	0
R Bowles	b Bevan	13	c and b Roden	9
E Williams	b Roden	4	b Roden	8
J Jones	b Roden	31	not out	75
F Rowlands	b Roden	0	b Stone	4
J Phillips	b Chippendale	6	caught b Roden	1
E James	ct b Roden	0	c and b Bevan	4
J Williams	ct b Roden	1	run out	3
D Davies	not out	0	st b Stone	1
C Green	hit wkt b Ram	0	b Stone	0
Extras	(byes 5)	5	(wides 9, byes 11)	20
Total		63		133

Ebbw Vale

Chippendale	ct b Williams	2	run out	1
Ram	ct Phillips b Jones	14	b Jones	21
Stone	b Hinton	11	b Hinton	3
Roden	b James	13	b Hinton	7
Bevan	b Jones	4	caught b Jones	6
R Roden	caught b Phillips	4	caught b Green	7
Williams	b Jones	6	lbw b Jones	2
Davies	caught b Jones	0	b Jones	0
James	run out	0	b Hinton	2

Trew	b Jones	1	b Hinton	0
Widdowson	caught b James	4	caught b James	0
Extras	(byes 6)	6	(byes 1)	1
Total		65		50

At this time, fixtures were relatively rare, because of the limited transport and cricket clubs often played games amongst their own members with their activities being similar to those of a modern-day golf club. In 1861 the Blaina team also played Rhymney as well as travelling twice to Newport to meet the United and the Commercials club. Away matches had become far easier following a number of transport improvements, especially the completion in 1850 of the Western Valley Branch of the Monmouthshire Railway and Canal Companies line from Blaina to Newport, followed nine years later by an extension to Nantyglo.

Duffryn Field (the old gasometer site), as it is today

The Blaina side in their inaugural matches in 1853 included several of the leading personnel at the local works, including Richard Bowles and Joseph Hinton, the surgeons at the Blaina ironworks; John Fothergill Rowlands, the 30 year-old owner of the Nantyglo foundry and Charles Widdowson, a Newcastle-born book-keeper employed at the Blaina works.

In 1856 they were joined by John Blasé, the superintendant of smiths, as well as some of the working men, including Ben Evans, a roller turner, and William Sewell, a warehouseman. The following year James Lanwarne, a labourer, and John Michael, a puddler, played in the match against Pontypool, whilst in 1861 Alfred Pasfield, a pattern maker, and Thomas Keen, a foundry worker, played against Newport Commercials and Newport United.

Some notable local residents also turned out including John Jones of Garnvach in 1853 plus John Jayne of Nantyglo a coal merchant and Justice of the Peace. The team in 1853 also included Edward James and James Phillips who were mineral agents, with their presence, and that of Jayne, showing how Levick used the playing of cricket as a means of fostering good relations with leading figures in the coal trade. Indeed, like all ironmasters he relied on the regular and abundant supply of cheap coal, and participation in cricket was a most novel way of creating effective and efficient relationships with the colliery personnel.

The Blaina side also included several leading people from the town, including a number of merchants and other members of Blaina's middle-class. For example in 1853, the team included Thomas Bevan, a local schoolmaster, plus David Davies, the owner of a tea merchant's shop in Hope Street. Tom Armstrong, the landlord of the Blaina Inn, appeared in 1857 and probably provided after-match sustenance, whilst in 1861 the team included Frederick Harris, the town's chemist and David Lewis, the owner of the local grocery

Frederick Levick's sons also appeared in the Blaina team, with George and Thomas each playing in 1861 against the Newport Commercials and Rhymney. Both were competent players, but neither were as skilful as their elder brother Frederick Carlton, who made his debut in 1856 against Tredegar and subsequently became one of leading young players in the northern part of the county appearing for a XXII of Monmouthshire against the All England Eleven at Newport in 1858, 1859 and 1860. In 1856 against Tredegar, Blaina also had the services of a guest, Douglas Onslow, an Indian-born gentleman, who was a good friend of Frederick Levick and played with him in 1858 and 1859 against the All England side.

But, after the boom years of the first half of the nineteenth century, the years from the 1850s onwards brought a steady decline in the iron trade. In particular, there was a decline in the use of the local ironstone following innovations in the production of steel as championed by Sir Henry Bessemer, with the Monmouthshire materials being unsuitable for the new process.

There were other problems as well affecting the Blaina area, not least in 1866 the spread of cholera throughout the region, forcing Levick and Simpson to close the works the following year. A measure of his high regard by the employees at the works can be gauged by the fact that that his staff raised a subscription and presented him with a testimonial to thank him for his sympathy and generosity. A group of trustees attempted to run the Works, but they closed operations in August 1867.

But it was only a brief stoppage as the following year a merger took place with the Nantyglo works and a new company called the Nantyglo and Blaina Iron Works Company came into being with Frederick Carlton Levick acting as general manager following the death of his distinguished father earlier in the year. Levick junior also had a thorough knowledge of the iron trade and the capabilities of the furnaces but, after a year or so of inactivity, the mills and forges were out of repair and in a state of general dilapidation. However, everyone pulled together and by 1869 a profit of £50,000 was achieved. In particular, the acquisition of the Nantyglo works meant that the running costs were reduced, with vast amounts of pig-iron being passed to Blaina for conversion to iron.

There were plans as well to build new coking ovens at Blaina, and to substitute steam power for the water balance system. Others suggested that the Works should diversify by selling coke, but these were quickly shelved as the availability of cheaper French and Belgian coal undercut the Blaina coke. A few small-scale expansions took place during the early 1870s but Levick was marginalised by the company's new directors, who possessed little technical know-how or knowledge of the local conditions. Levick advised his new bosses to increase the production of finished iron at Blaina with materials from Nantyglo, where the supplies of coal were plentiful enough to power the local furnaces and provide a decent surplus which could be sold. But the Nantyglo workers feared that their works would soon be closed if all of the advanced smelting took place at Blaina and, after strenuous representations from the Nantyglo works, Levick's proposals were thrown out.

It proved to be the wrong decision as over the course of the next few years, labour unrest characterised events at Blaina, with the employees – like their counterparts at Dowlais – going on strike in the pursuit of higher wages. Ironically, some of Levick's proposals were belatedly introduced in a bid to reduce costs but, with the position not improving, the Nantyglo and Blaina Iron Works Company ceased operations in March 1874, principally through bad management and a failure to act on advice from the men who really knew the iron trade and local conditions. To meet the demands of their creditors, the whole of the machinery, engines, railway lines and every bit of iron that could be found was sold. By 1878 the works had been completely dismantled and the buildings were left in a dilapidated state. The local pits stayed open but, with people leaving the area because of the closure of the ironworks, it was no surprise that the cricketing activities of the Blaina club also ceased.

Some matches had been staged in the early 1870s with George and Thomas Levick organising as well as playing in matches against Ebbw Vale in 1870, Crickhowell in 1872, and Crumlin in both 1872 and 1873. Once again, the Blaina side included workers from the Ironworks, including John Hazlehurst Donne, a clerk born in Buenos Aires in Argentina, and Nathaniel Merriman, another clerk who had moved to the area from his native Cheshire. Also in the side was James Wallen, the owner of a boot-making business in High Street, as well as John Hale, a local publican.

The Levicks were also fortunate enough to secure the services of some prominent cricketers, including Bertie Young, a Neath-born engineer who played for the Glamorganshire side in 1870 as well as Breconshire in 1872. Young had initially worked for the Vale of Neath Railway before being appointed to work at Crumlin on the famous iron bridge which was opened in June 1857 to carry the Taff Vale extension to the Newport, Abergavenny and Hereford Railway, which at 200 feet high was the highest railway viaduct in the U.K. The Levicks had business contacts with businesses in Crumlin, which was situated at the northern end of the Monmouthshire Canal and was one of the outlets from which iron from Blaina and Nantyglo was sent to the docks at Newport. Despite working at Crumlin, Young appeared for the Blaina side against Crumlin in the matches in the early 1870s. Young was also a member of the South Wales CC, the first regional side to represent the region, and undertook an annual tour to London to play matches against leading sides in the Home Counties. Having Young's services was a major coup for the Levicks and highlighted both the strength and depth of their business, political and cricketing contacts.

But Young was just one of many prominent cricketers whom George Levick had contact with. Another example of his importance in sporting circles came at the end of May 1871 when he assembled a star-studded eleven which met the Cardiff club at the Arms Park in a two-day contest – described by *The Cardiff Times* as "Cardiff's first importance match of the season". Indeed, Levick's eleven included many of the movers and shakers in South Walian cricket at that time, including Arthur Redwood, the solicitor who lived at Bassaleg House and who played for the Glamorganshire, Monmouthshire and Breconshire county sides as well as the South Wales CC, as well as fellow solicitor William Randall, who also appeared for the Glamorganshire side and was a major figure with the Bridgend and Merthyr Mawr clubs.

Also in Levick's eleven was Thomas Jotham, the owner of the Cardiff-based drapers business and a leading figure in the politics in the town, plus his Cardiff colleague Edmund Barber who was a civil engineer and played for a number of county sides including Glamorganshire, Monmouthshire and Shropshire, besides the West Gloucestershire club which had close links with WG Grace and his family. Perhaps the Levicks hoped that by having contact with well-connected cricketers, they could organise matches for the Blaina side against some of the leading clubs in South Wales and in the West Country. But this was not to be as the closure of the ironworks dealt a massive blow to the local economy, and led to the demise of the initial Blaina club whose last known match took place on June 18th 1873 at Newbridge against the Crumlin Viaduct Works.

2
THE SECOND CLUB

After several years of inactivity, Blaina cricket club re-formed in the mid-1880s. By this time, the ironworks had re-opened as a tinplate works, and in 1881 the Blaina Iron and Tin Plate Company employed 1,300 people. Coal mining also thrived at this time with a number of new pits being sunk. For example, Griffin's who had sunk their first pit in 1873 opened two more in 1882. North Blaina Colliery, sunk in 1860 by the Nantyglo and Blaina Company, also expanded their operations, whilst the Henwaun Pit, sunk in 1857 by Crawshay Bailey, also had several new pits having become the property of John Lancaster and Company in 1881. As a result, around 861,000 tons of coal was sent each year from the Blaina pits to Newport during the 1880s.

The upswing in the local economy meant that the number of people living in Blaina increased and in 1884 the Blaina Central School opened. The resurgence in industrial activity boosted other sports with the influx of tinplate workers leading to the creation of a rugby side. The game had been first played in the town in the mid 1870s onwards following the arrival of a group of iron and tinplate workers from Llanelli. In particular, Alf James and Sid Lewis brought not only industrial skills but a knowledge of rugby football. Formal clubs were established around 1875, with the town's industrialists also offering encouragement and financial help believing, once again, it was beneficial for the workers to be involved in organised sport. Indeed, one of the earliest teams was called Ironsides. But, with a slump in the iron trade and the closure of the Blaina works, the rugby players approached some of the colliery owners for their support. One in particular, Sidney Lancaster was most helpful and helped the Blaina club to purchase a ground in 1877.

Blaina Cricket's Rugby-playing Stars

Over the years many Blaina cricketers have turned out for the town's rugby club. This trend started in the late 1870s and early 1880s with one of the earliest stars being Tom Clapp, the London-born son of a local doctor, who had learnt the rudiments of cricket and rugby whilst a pupil at Monmouth School.

> Clapp captained Blaina RFC in the 1880/81 season, before going on to join the Newport club – one of the top sides in South Wales – and winning 14 Welsh rugby caps between 1882 and 1888. Clapp was no mean cricketer either, playing with much success for the Newport club, besides appearing for the Next XVIII against the South Wales CC at the Rodney Parade ground in June 1886. Had he not emigrated to the United States in the late 1880s, Clapp would surely have joined several of his rugby-playing colleagues in the Monmouthshire side – created in 1890 – or even the Glamorgan side when they became a Minor County in 1897.
>
> In more recent times, David Watkins is amongst the stars of the oval ball game to have played cricket for Blaina. Born in the town in 1942 and educated at Cwmcelyn School, he performed with credit as a fast bowler during the mid 1960s before moving to Northern England as a rugby league professional. He had previously won 21 caps playing rugby union for Wales and had been on the British Lions tour to New Zealand in 1966, but the following year he joined Salford and subsequently became the first person to have captained both the British Lions as well as the Great Britain Rugby League team – a fine achievement for a Blaina cricketer!

The Blaina cricket club re-formed in the 1880s and, by the end of the decade, they were staging home and away matches against neighbouring industrial centres of Rhymney, Brynmawr, Abercarn, Abertillery, Pontymister, Tredegar and the Beaufort club from Ebbw Vale. They still retained the ambition of the previous club and were quite prepared to travel some distance to play some of the leading clubs. In July 1887 they travelled to Cardiff to play the St. Mary's side from Cardiff whilst, in July 1889, they attempted to organise a match with the Swansea club to coincide with the visit of the Blaina Co-operative Society to the West Wales town.

Like other teams in the Monmouthshire valleys, matches were also staged against some of the junior clubs in the Newport area, and from late morning on Saturdays, the trains heading south were often crammed with cricketers and their supporters. For instance, on one Saturday in 1889 the Blaina side travelled to Tydu at Newport to play the Nettlefold's side at the Castle Works and were joined at Risca by members of the North Risca team who were playing Newport United and then later the Abercarn side who were en route to play Maindee.

Whilst the trains were highly convenient, any delays with the services led to a number of knock-on effects, such as in 1889 when the Abercarn side were attempting to reach Blaina to start a match at 2pm. However, it was not

THE HISTORY OF BLAINA CRICKET CLUB

Blaina railway station

until after 4pm that they arrived, by which time several of the Blaina side had departed, believing that the match would not go ahead. Several members of the Abertillery club, who were without a fixture, had been more successful in their travelling and having decided to visit Blaina to watch the match, they were at the ground when the Abercarn side eventually arrived. Their presence was fortuitous as a combined Blaina and Abertillery XI was hastily put together as the match belatedly started.

However, it continued to be quite an eventful contest as, shortly after 6pm, the game abruptly ended with the combined side on 42/4. The cause was a heated dispute over the decisions made by the Abercarn umpire. Having previously turned down a series of appeals when the combined side were bowling, he was now upholding every shout from his team. Percy Martin, the Blaina captain called in his batsmen and refused to continue with the match.

Martin was one of several staff from the Henwaun pit to be closely associated with the club, with the new organisation during the 1880s having a close affiliation with the collieries owned by John Lancaster and Company, with John Dakers, the Durham-born general manager of the Henwaun Pit, acting as the Club's President. Martin was one of the mechanics at the mine, but his association with the Blaina club abruptly ended at the end of the 1889 season when he was promoted to a senior post at the Panteg works.

Another person closely associated with the colliery was Club secretary Robert Norfolk, a Nottingham-born gentleman who was the transport manager at Lancaster's pit. Brothers Mark and Silas Robbins, who had each

THE SECOND CLUB

Blaina railway sidings in the early 1900s

migrated from Somerset to work at the Henwaun pit, were also regulars for the side, with Mark showing great promise with the bat whilst Silas was a handy seam bowler. The side at this time also regularly included some of the staff from the Blaina Iron and Tin Plate Company, including opening batsman Stephen Winmill and Robert Meyrick, who were both tinplate workers. Dr. J. Hawker Soper, the surgeon at the Works, was also one of the Club's Vice-Presidents.

Unlike the initial club, the teams chosen by the new organisation rarely included guests or prominent figures in local politics who were enthusiastic, if modest, performers with bat or ball. Leading members of local society were involved in an off-field role, with the Club's Vice-Presidents including the Rev Howell Howells, the vicar of St. Peter's church in Blaina, whilst the committee included Joseph Parry, the Head of Blaina Boy's School who encouraged his young charges to take part in healthy recreation. Indeed, it was probably the result of Parry's encouragement that from 1889 the Blaina Club arranged fixtures for their Junior XI containing boys and young students from the area. One of these was a student attending St. David's College, Lampeter

THE HISTORY OF BLAINA CRICKET CLUB

Joseph Parry

called Danny Sproule, who was the eldest son of Henry, the Headmaster of Garnvach Boys School. Born in Blaina in 1869, Danny was a talented left-arm spinner as he showed in 1889 when he took 9/11 against Tredegar.

The early 1890s saw the formation of other sporting organisations in Blaina, including in 1890 the creation of a tennis club as well as Blaina Rangers association football club. But this period also witnessed a change to the composition, organisation and name of the Blaina cricket club, prompted by Percy Martin's departure at the end of the 1889 season and the loss of the field, owned by Lancaster's, which the club had previously used. The area was needed for other uses from 1890 and the loss of Lancaster's patronage affected the Blaina club.

The ties with Lancaster's lessened for the next few years as a side called Blaina "A" as they were described in the local newspapers between 1890 and 1892, filled the void. The new secretary was Harry Gunter, a locally-born colliery clerk who was in his early twenties, whilst the treasurer was a Wiltshire-born miner called Morgan Trew. Two other miners – the Sperring brothers from Somerset – were also the club's leading bowlers at this time, whilst the side also included another collier in Staffordshire-born Moses Eynon. Several of the workers at the Blaina Iron and Tin Plate Company also appeared on a regular basis including father and son, John and James Hinkin who had moved to the area from Carmarthenshire, whilst Somerset-born steelworker Alfred Sandy served on the committee, all adding to an air of a club full of workingmen rather than containing businessmen, toffs or leaders of local society, besides showing the importance of in-migration and the arrival of Englishmen.

Their fixture list was less extensive, both numerically and geographically, with games against Abertillery, Beaufort. Ebbw Vale Stars, Brynmawr and Tredegar Lillywhites. There are no records of lengthier journeys to Newport and the loss of Lancaster's patronage affected the club's finances, causing them to concentrate their activities in the local area. The side also participated in the Bat Competition organised by the Abertillery Town club – described in the local press as Blaina Juniors, the side however contained most of the men who played for the Blaina A side, although as most were in their twenties, the description Juniors was probably apt.

THE SECOND CLUB

Garnvach CC from the 1890s

Their games in this competition were also marred by disputes over the umpiring with their semi-final contest at Abertillery in 1891 being retrospectively declared a no-result after Blaina had narrowly won the initial game by four runs. The organising committee ordered a re-match at Blaina, with the offer of being able to take half the gate receipts, which helped persuade the Blaina club to agree with the decision. Some felt that the committee had no right to change the outcome, but as it turned out the Abertillery Juniors were bundled out for just 25 as Blaina won by four wickets. Their reward was a final against the Ebbw Vale Stars who they dismissed for just 40. It continued to be a low-scoring contest as the Blaina side slipped to 35/7, but their tail-enders could not pull off a dramatic victory as the Ebbw Vale side won by two runs.

There might, though, have been more than just the loss of senior staff at Lancaster's Pit behind the emergence of the Blaina A side as some of the leading players from Blaina in the 1880s switched allegiance to other clubs, most notably the Robbins brothers who moved to Abertillery and Danny Sproule who, together with his younger brother Arthur, played in the Nantyglo side in 1891 and 1892. In the latter season, he played in the local derby at Blaina but

THE HISTORY OF BLAINA CRICKET CLUB

Garnvach CC in the early 1900s

Sproule's spin bowling could not see Nantyglo to victory as George Sperring's seam bowling won the game for the Blaina A side.

In 1893 a Blaina town side was re-formed with a quite extensive programme of fixtures, including games against Abercarn, Abertillery 2nd XI, Beaufort, Blaenavon, Garnvach, Gilwern, Newbridge and Tredegar. Several of the players from the 1880s had moved on or had been poached, so there was plenty of fresh blood in both the on-field and off-field affairs of the club with George Morris, a clerk at Lancaster's pit acting as secretary, with Robert Page, a carpenter born in Tiverton, Devon serving as treasurer. Amongst the new players to appear were colliers John Cannon from Lancashire and William Hathaway who had been born in Risca, together with locally-born Henry Maidment who worked with his father driving the steam engines at the colliery. Other notables from Blaina also participated with the club with the town's doctor, Henry Bevan, acting as the Club's President.

The following year John Dakers – the general manager of Lancaster's – announced that the colliery would closely support the club as, from May 1894 at a meeting held in the Reading Institute, the side became known as Blaina Lancaster. A modest injection of cash also followed, allowing club members to share new and improved equipment, as well as having a larger supply of bats and, most importantly of all, balls. Robert Norfolk was elected as club captain, whilst Robert Meyrick and Harry Gunter were appointed onto the committee. James Owen, a clerk at the Lancaster pit, was also elected as

THE SECOND CLUB

Nantyglo Primitive Methodists

club secretary, with fixtures secured against Abertillery, Nantyglo Wesleyans and Govilion. However, the greatest fillip for the new club was that Danny Sproule, together with his brothers Arthur and James, agreed to play for the Blaina side, with Danny playing a major role with the ball as the Nantyglo side were defeated by 11 runs.

In June 1895 the Blaina Lancaster side met an eleven drawn from the other teams in the town. The combined side duly won by 9 runs in a closely fought contest which showcased the depth of cricketing talent within the area. At this time, a Blaina United and Blaina Cemetary side were also in existence, as well as several chapel and church teams, all showing the extent to which cricket was being played in the industrial town – something which proved to be a major benefit for the ongoing development of cricket within Monmouthshire.

3
THE RISE OF MONMOUTHSHIRE AND THE CREATION OF CENTRAL PARK

The last two decades of the nineteenth century were boom years for cricket in general in Monmouthshire, with the rise in the number of thriving clubs leading to the formation of a county club which subsequently emulated the feats of neighbours Glamorgan by entering the Minor County Championship in 1901.

An eleven, variously described as the Gentlemen of Monmouthshire and the Monmouthshire Butterflies had been created in the early 1880s, with its leading protagonists being Edward Curre of Itton Court, Chepstow and solicitor Arthur Redwood who lived at Bassaleg House. It was though, largely a gentlemen's eleven playing country house matches at such palatial locations as Tredegar House near Newport and Merthyr Mawr House near Bridgend, rather than being a side which was representative of the amateur talent throughout the county.

This changed in 1890 following the creation of the Monmouthshire County Cricket Association by Fred Phillips, a member of the well-known Newport brewing family. Born in Stony Stratford in 1857 and educated at Millbrook School in Hampshire. Phillips had been a member of the South Wales CC which had disbanded in 1886 with the chief objective that its regional representatives went away to form county clubs. Merchants and social leaders in Cardiff and Swansea led the way by creating Glamorgan CCC in 1888 and, keen not to be upstaged by their business rivals, Phillips set about creating a fully fledged county organisation for Monmouthshire which unlike the earlier teams was truly representative of cricket throughout the county.

A series of trial matches were organised at Newport during May 1890, including a game between East and West Monmouthshire, with the latter eleven including Mark Robbins, who had learnt his cricket at Blaina and was now a star player with Abertillery, whom he led in 1894. Besides being a talented batsman, Robbins was also a capable wicket-keeper and, in August, he was chosen as the Monmouthshire wicket-keeper for their match against

Glamorgan at Newport. It proved to be a match to remember for the former Blaina player as he was at the crease when the winning runs were secured as Monmouthshire won by two wickets.

All concerned with the Monmouthshire club realised that this was just the first of many steps towards a successful county side, and the county's hierarchy were aware that a lot of hard work was needed at club level to ensure that the cream of talent rose to the top. An inter-club competition was therefore instigated and in 1895 Blaina accepted an invitation to take part in the challenge, realising how beneficial it would be for both club and county. It proved to be a chastening experience for the town side as they were firstly defeated by Abertillery by 205 runs, with their former player Silas Robbins making 80, whilst Henry Steele notched up 88, before a second defeat to Cwmcarn by 40 runs ended Blaina's interest in the Monmouthshire Challenge Cup.

Nevertheless, Blaina continued to participate in the competition in 1896, with matches against Abertillery, Cwmcarn and Machen. The contest against Abertillery once again saw Blaina come up against some of their former stars, with Stephen Winmill making an unbeaten 87 as Abertillery declared on 180/5 before dismissing Blaina for just 8 in the space of nine action-packed overs, with seven batsmen failing to trouble the scorers as Silas Robbins took the remarkable figures of 8/7. The other games in the competition saw Blaina record resounding victories as they defeated Cwmcarn and Machen, with the latter dismissed for just 21 in reply to Blaina's 101 with the last six wickets falling in succession without a run being scored as Griffith Abraham, a locally-born schoolteacher, returned figures of 8/10.

In July 1896 Robert Norfolk was instrumental in assembling a Blaina and District XI to play Crickhowell, with the man from Lancaster's pit negotiating with a number of the other sides in the area in order to field as strong a side as possible. Norfolk himself, together with Samuel Francis, Griffith Abraham and Arthur Sproule played for the combined XI. It proved to be the last major action by Norfolk as, at the end of the season, the colliery traffic manager left South Wales to take up a similar appointment in Beeston, Nottinghamshire. The Blaina club also lost the services of bowler Tom Davies, who had taught for several years at Blaina Boys School before securing a more lucrative appointment in London.

In 1898 another important innovation took place in the development of cricket in Monmouthshire with the creation of an inter-club league run, as the *South Wales Gazette* described "on similar lines to the one now in vogue in rugby football." The seeds for the formation of a Monmouthshire League were sown at a meeting held in April 1898 at the Wilkins Temperance Hotel in Abertillery. Present at the meeting were representatives from the Abertillery, Abertillery Wesleyan, Beaufort, Nantyglo and Blaina clubs and, according

Garnvach CC in 1904

to the *Gazette*, all were "unanimously of the opinion that the formation of a league would give a decided impetus to the popular summer pastime."

David Boswell, a major figure with the Abertillery club and an insurance agent in the town, agreed to act as Chairman of the new organisation, with Stephen Winmill agreeing to act as interim Secretary. The former Blaina batsman was succeeded by another Abertillery man shortly before the League fixtures got underway in mid-May. By this time, Blaenavon, Crumlin and Cwmtillery had also joined the League, with letters of invitation being sent to other clubs. The only entry requirements were a fee of five shillings and being "in possession of a suitable ground." The latter criterion ended Nantyglo's participation as in, mid-season, their ground was taken over for industrial purposes and, with no suitable alternative, they had to withdraw from the competition.

The Abertillery men who formed the core of the new League's administration were clearly very ambitious men as they suggested that a similar League should be created in the eastern valleys, with an annual play-off against the top side from their western-based League to determine the county champions. They also made contact with Foster Stedman, the captain and secretary of the Monmouthshire county side and, to their delight, the Suffolk-born batsman agreed to serve on the committee and to assemble a county XI to play a League XI. Stedman, who was the land agent to the Tredegar Estate, was perhaps the most influential figure in Monmouthshire cricket and it was a feather in the cap of the Abertillery men to secure his support.

Blaina's inaugural match in the new League took place on May 13th when they travelled to Blaenavon, but a steady innings by Tom Gabb laid the foundations for a 47-run victory. In mid-June Blaina gained a major scalp as they beat Abertillery with vice-captain Richard Jones claiming 4/22 and Frank Benger, a Somerset-born collier, returning figures of 3/9 as Blaina won by 17 runs. Although Griffith Abraham had joined the Garn-Nantyglo side, Arthur Sproule was available for Blaina who for much of the season could field a useful side. Sam Francis proved himself to be a very capable opening batsman, whilst Club captain Tom Cannon enjoyed a productive season with the ball. With Tom Davies available in his school holidays, Blaina finished a highly creditable second in the new League, behind winners Abertillery Wesleyans. Davies, together with Gabb were also chosen in the League XI which met Stedman's Monmouthshire side at Abertillery in early September.

An Ordnance Survey map of the Blaina area from 1901

THE HISTORY OF BLAINA CRICKET CLUB

The site of Blaina Recreation Ground where the Blaina cricketers played until the creation of Central Park shortly before the Great War. It has subsequently been developed as building land

Although the county side won by 144 runs, the match was evidence of the growing strength of the clubs in the Western Valleys.

1899 proved to be a summer to forget for Blaina – although Tom Cannon took 8 wickets in the 17-run victory over Blaenavon, the club finished bottom of the table and failed to win another game all summer in the League competition. The summer though did witness the emergence of two other teams in the town – Blaina Congregationals and Blaina West End. The latter met the town club at the start of the 1900 season in what proved to be a very one-sided contest and an easy victory for the Blaina club, "premiers" as they were described in the *Gazette*. The victory appears to have put the Blaina side in good heart for their contest against Abertillery which they won by three runs thanks to a stubborn innings from captain Will Lloyd. It proved to be a far more successful summer with Blaina meeting Abertillery in mid-September at Beaufort in a contest to determine the outcome of the League title. The Robbins brothers had a decent afternoon with bat and ball for Abertillery and their efforts proved decisive as their side won by 48 runs to lift the title.

There were some clouds on the horizon, with the first concerning the future of the Blaina Recreation Grounds with the Pyle and Blaina Mining Company showing interest in purchasing the area as a site for new spoil tips. The town's sportsmen made their feelings known about the potential loss of the Recreation Grounds, whilst the Blaina Licensed Victuallers Association made it known that they were also keen to purchase the fields so that sports could continue. As it turned out the Mining Company did not proceed with their bid to purchase the area, thanks to the influence of George Roche, a London-born administrator at the Works and a decent batsman with the town club.

The second cloud though, related to the future participation of Blaina in the Monmouthshire League. They met with little success in 1901, with the nadir coming in the game against Abertillery when they were dismissed for just 9. Although Richard Jones took a hat-trick against Abertillery and 8/9 in the 29-run victory over Ebbw Vale, there was a general feeling that, with the club having a rising debt, it would be better for the club to withdraw from the League and play some of the local teams rather than the premier sides. The League competition however had served its purpose in helping to raise the standard of club cricket within the county to the benefit of the Monmouthshire Club who in 1901 were elevated to the Minor County Championship – a sign of the coming of age of cricket in the county.

The early 1900s were a period of consolidation for Blaina CC under the captaincy of Tom Davies with the club's financial position having improved sufficiently to allow regular games against the likes of Bargoed, Blaenavon, Brynmawr, Cross Keys, Cwmcarn, Nantyglo and Rhymney. The decade saw the club make forward strides with 1908 being a particularly successful summer with just one defeat and handsome victories over Abertillery and Tredegar.

Some of the old stagers still did their bit for the club's onward development, including Frank Benger who took 5/13 against Pontnewynydd in 1902, as well as seven wickets against Abertillery in 1908, but it was a number of new faces who made the greatest impression for the Blaina club who now had colliery proprietor Matthew Wolstenholme as their President. One of the new players to make an impact for the 1st XI was Bert Reddiford who made a composed 38 against Tredegar and took 4/5 in the contest against Pontnewynydd in 1903, with the following year taking a hat-trick against Crickhowell.

For a short period, William England, the former Abertillery seam bowler, had a couple of seasons with Blaina, during which he took 5/8 in the contest with Crickhowell in 1903. However, for much of this decade the most successful bowler was Charlie Hillier, a Somerset-born cobbler, who claimed 5/11 in the plum fixture against Crickhowell in 1903, besides taking seven wickets in 1907 against both Bargoed and Newbridge, as well as six wickets against Blaenavon in the same season. Also in the wickets was Vaughan Chaffey, a young coal trimmer born in Abersychan, who took five wickets in the matches against Brynmawr and Abertillery in 1907.

THE HISTORY OF BLAINA CRICKET CLUB

Duffryn Field in 1918

Another new face was Harold Law, a young coal trimmer who had made his debut in 1903, the year after he had been appointed the founding captain of a Blaina United side who also secured the patronage of James Lancaster. 1903 also saw a team called Blaina Primitive Methodists take to the field, whilst in 1906 a club was formed at Winchestown, followed in 1908 by a Blaina Salemites XI. With so many cricketers in the area, the Blaina club organised a match from 1904 against a Blaina and District XI as well as having regular fixtures with the Blaina United club, who beat the town club by 8 runs in 1907.

In 1908 the Blaina United side joined the Western Valleys Cricket League, playing a host of other junior teams including Aberbeeg, Brynmawr Celts, Beaufort Lillywhites, Ebbw Vale Coronets, Ebbw Vale Methodists, Garnvach, Llanhilleth 2nd XI and Winchestown. The same summer also saw the Blaina United team, together with guests Frank Benger and Charlie Hillier, visit Somerset and Wiltshire on a ten-day tour in August. Two games were played against Frome, in addition to matches against Chapmanslade, Midsomer Norton, Westbury and the Bath Association.

The tour was a massive success and in 1909 the Blaina Lancaster Town Club, to give them their full name, and the Blaina United side joined forces with the Blaina Touring Club, repeating the visit of the previous year, with additional matches against Nunney, Warminster and Longleat. Led by Tom Davies, the combined side met with success, with Vaughan Chaffey also taking a hat-trick against Midsomer Norton.

MONMOUTHSHIRE AND CENTRAL PARK

TL Davies

The Blaina cricketers at Frome in 1910. Back row – David Pritchard, Jack Jones, Sam Jones, Tim Williams, Dan Jelly, Len Chaffey. Front row – Vaughan Chaffey, E. Hathaway, Dorset Williams, Tom Lloyd Davies, Jim Davies, W. Rogers, Tom Taylor and Charlie Hillier

The Creation of Central Park

1909 was a landmark summer for the Blaina club as it saw the club play for the final time at the Recreation Grounds as, after a few years of uncertainty, plans were put forward by the District Council for the creation of a new recreation ground to serve the thriving town.

Like other District Councils across South Wales, there had been concern for many years over the provision of recreational facilities for the local residents. A few enlightened landowners, such as Lord Tredegar in Newport, had generously given land for public parks and recreation grounds, but in the industrial valleys little thought had been given to the welfare of the residents. In the early 1900s some District Councils started to apportion land for recreational purposes, and in 1909 work began on establishing a permanent home for both Blaina rugby and cricket clubs, in addition to creating a bowls green and pleasure garden.

Central Park was formally opened on May 13th, 1910 when Blaina met the powerful Hills Plymouth side from Merthyr. The visitors had three professionals in their ranks, fielding batsman Arthur Webb who had played for Hampshire from 1895 until 1904; Richard Davey, a promising batsman who had spent time on the Surrey groundstaff, and the veteran left-arm seam bowler Frederick Roberts between 1887 and 1905. The Merthyr side proved too strong, winning the game by 105 runs but, despite the defeat, it was a very jolly occasion for the Blaina club with the Lancaster Town Band playing on the outfield during the tea interval and entertaining the sizeable crowd.

The Central Park square

1910 proved to be a very successful one for the Blaina club, especially their bowlers, with Vaughan Chaffey creating a new club record by taking over 100 wickets, reaching the century mark towards the end of a memorable summer in the match against a Blaina and District XI at Central Park. It was a vintage season for the 27 year-old from Abersychan with his record haul of wickets included 7/18 in the home victory over Blackwood and six wickets in the away wins against Newbridge and Abergavenny. Charlie Hiller enjoyed much success as well taking six-wicket hauls against Blaenavon and Brynmawr whilst young all-rounder Ivor Jones took six wickets in the victory at Blackwood and won selection to the Monmouthshire Colts side. The Blaina touring club also enjoyed a highly successful tour to Somerset and Wiltshire during the August Bank Holiday, with victories against Beckington, Peasedown, Midsomer Norton, Longleat and Chapmanslade, with the latter game taking place in the lavish grounds of Mr. Phipps, the MP for Westbury.

THE HISTORY OF BLAINA CRICKET CLUB

Duffryn Field

The new wicket at Central Park also proved to be superior to the previous one in the Recreation Grounds, making the Blaina club the envy of the junior clubs in the locality who still had to use whatever land they could find. Besides helping to raise the identity of the Blaina club, it also helped the club recruit new players, including one – EW Watkins – who was to play a major role in the onward development of Blaina Cricket Club.

4
THE ARRIVAL OF EVAN WATKINS

One name is written large in the affairs of Blaina CC either side of the Great War – that of EW Watkins. Born in Merthyr Tydfil in September 1882, Evan William Watkins began playing both rugby and cricket for Abertillery in his late-teens and swiftly met with much success. Indeed, by the mid 1900s Watkins was one of the leading young sportsmen in Monmouthshire, winning a national bowling competition after taking 8/1 against Ebbw Vale in 1906 and playing county rugby.

Watkins' was also a talented winger with Abertillery RFC, scoring 23 tries, besides playing with distinction for several senior clubs, including London Welsh, Gloucester, Lydney and Tredegar, whilst he was also given a chance to appear in the Newport team – one of the crack sides at the time – but he declined the offer. His exploits on the rugby field soon attracted the attention of the Welsh selectors, who in December 1907 selected the engineering student in one of the teams that took part in the Welsh trial at the Rodney Parade ground in Newport. A decent performance led to his selection in the second trial at Pontypool, but the match never took place as the ground was frozen.

Evan Watkins

His swift running and excellent ball-handling skills also drew the attention of scouts from several rugby league clubs who were scouring the Welsh valleys for prospective talent. Indeed, Watkins was one of many promising players who were being courted by rugby league clubs and being offered sizeable sums to turn professional. The offers were very attractive especially as several economic and labour problems were starting to affect the mining valleys. The cost of coal rose as companies were forced to use deeper seams of coal, often in challenging geological conditions. Wages however failed to rise, and from 1906 onwards there were several disputes about the working conditions underground and the notion of a guaranteed minimum wage led to many disputes with the colliery owners denting the previously harmonious relationship which had generally existed during the more prosperous Victorian era.

The heads of many talented young players were being turned by the generous offers from the scouts, both from the northern clubs as well as the professional clubs formed in Aberdare, Barry, Ebbw Vale, Merthyr and Treherbert. The latter clubs however had been viewed with suspicion by many in the Welsh rugby community which hitherto had been exclusively amateur. Indeed, these feelings led one commentator to claim how "there will be a revulsion of feeling against the mongrel game that the professionals have introduced."

Nevertheless, a New Zealand professional side visited Wales in 1907/08 and in January their match against a Welsh side at Aberdare drew a crowd of 10,000. With several other young players accepting lucrative offers, Watkins accepted an offer from the Warrington Rugby League club on January 21st, 1908. His signing-on fee was a handsome £180, whilst his match terms were £3 10 shillings per game. Warrington also agreed to assist Watkins with his engineering studies, securing him a post at a nearby electrical plant and, despite the negative comments from those who believed rugby was an amateur game, Watkins headed north believing that the experience would set him up for life.

Warrington were one of the leading lights in the northern game. In 1895 they had been one of the twenty-one clubs which met at The George Hotel in Huddersfield at which the Northern Rugby Union was created. In 1906/07 they had also proposed a switch in the format of the game from fifteen players to thirteen-a-side which, together with suggestions for other rule changes, they believed would speed up the game. These proposals were subsequently adopted as 1907 became a pivotal season for Warrington as they won the Challenge Cup Final, defeating Oldham, followed in the autumn by a victory over the New Zealand tourists.

Warrington also had generous sponsorship from the Greenall Whitley Brewery and, with the new format of the game, they were looking for fresh talent and speedy backs. Evan Watkins fitted the bill perfectly and in February 1908 he played for Warrington A against Egerton – a match watched by 4,000, most of whom were eager to see the promising Welshman in action. It was a dream debut for the young Welshman who scored two tries and was chaired off the field by the delighted supporters. The following week he made his

THE ARRIVAL OF EVAN WATKINS

Berea Chapel – seen around 1915

debut for Warrington in their away match against Bradford Northern, and in the next couple of months, Watkins scored five tries in the next eight games.

A bright future was being predicted for the young Welshman but his professional career ended on April 17th, 1908 when the winger sustained a leg injury in Warrington's home match with Leeds. Sadly, he was never to play professional rugby again and returned to South Wales looking to regain fitness and also resurrect his cricketing career. His return was greeted largely with delight by the cricketing community of Abertillery, with Watkins taking a hat-trick in the match against Panteg in 1909 and winning a place in the Monmouthshire side for their Minor County matches against Devon, Carmarthenshire and Cornwall. Warrington had kept his registration for the 1909/1910 season in the hope that Watkins would be fit enough to return north, but the medical advice was that his leg – whilst being fine for playing cricket – would not stand up to further heavy contact in rugby, and his professional career came to an abrupt end.

With his studies having ended, Watkins secured an engineering post in the Blaina area and, to the delight of the Central Park club, he switched his allegiances to the town club. Watkins had been impressed by the quality of the wicket and, after his disappointments at Warrington, and perhaps a little bit of jealousy from others in Abertillery about his lucrative deal with the rugby league club, he was keen to make a fresh start now that his rugby playing days had ended. He made his debut in late July against a Western Valley League XI, and after Vaughan Chaffey had taken five wickets against the combined side, Watkins made an impressive 36* at number three as he eased his new side to a seven wicket victory.

A few weeks later he opened the batting for Blaina at Abertillery where his batting skills helped to set up another victory with Watkins opening the batting and top-scoring with 46 as Blaina won by 24 runs. His first half-century for the club came a few weeks later against Pontlottyn as he made 58 out of Blaina's total of 82 – a score which proved far too much for the Pontlottyn side against Blaina's vibrant bowling attack who clinically guided their side to a 53-run victory. Watkins' good form for Blaina led to his inclusion in the Monmouthshire side which played Glamorgan in both 1910 and 1911. However, he met with little success in either contest, both of which resulted in a heavy defeat for the Monmouthshire side.

1911 was a red letter year for the Blaina club as wicket-keeper Tom Taylor became their first centurion, making an unbeaten 101 against Blaenavon at Central Park, much to the delight of a decent-sized crowd. In all, he struck 14 fours and a six as his efforts saw Blaina ease to victory by the mammoth margin of 152 runs. This was one of nineteen victories out of the 23 matches staged in 1911, with Vaughan Chaffey and Ivor Jones continuing to be amongst the best bowling partnerships in the Western Valleys. One of the highlights was Chaffey's eight wickets against Blaenavon, whilst once again he also enjoyed success on the annual tour to Frome and Westbury. In 1911 the Blaina tourists were joined by a reasonable number of supporters who also participated in musical entertainment after the games, with the "Cymric Glee Party" as they were known, being most favourably received in the market towns and villages of Somerset and Wiltshire.

Work commitments prevented Evan Watkins from playing regularly for Blaina in the years leading up to the outbreak of the Great War but, when he did get an opportunity to play, there was no doubting his class, such as in 1911 when he posted an unbeaten 56 against Harry Cockcroft's Newport XI with his batting, plus Will England's five-wicket haul seeing Blaina to a 101-run victory.

In 1912 Blaina accepted an invitation to join the West Monmouthshire and District Cricket Combination and for the years leading up to the First World War, Tom Davies' team continued to enjoy much success thanks to the bowling of Ivor Jones and Vaughan Chaffey. In 1912 Jones claimed seven wickets in the win against Ebbw Vale, six against Tredegar and five against Abergavenny, whilst in the same year Chaffey recorded six-wicket hauls against Ynysddu and Cockcroft's XI, with the latter game seeing the Newport

THE ARRIVAL OF EVAN WATKINS

Blaina Congregationals CC

men skittled out for 13. In 1913 Chaffey set yet another club record by taking 10/15 against Ynysddu, whilst in 1914 he took wickets against Crickhowell as the Powys side were dismissed for 26, followed a few weeks later by a seven-wicket haul at Brynmawr.

With all going well on the field, the only cloud was over the rents levied by the District Council for the use of Central Park. During 1912 the Council suggested that the Town club should be charged £7 per annum for using the Park with the United side being charged £3 p.a. and the rugby club £15 p.a. Whilst the rugby side were able to afford this sum, the two cricket sides were in a far less happy position. In 1912 the Town club only raised £31 8s through gate receipts, whilst the United side had an income of just £2 15s in gates. The Council's proposals were simply too high and a huge sigh of relief was expressed when a revised proposal of £3 3s was agreed upon.

Darker clouds though were looming in Europe, and the outbreak of the First World War brought an abrupt end to Blaina's cricketing activity on Central Park in early August 1914. A few fund-raising matches were staged in the course of the next four summers, but it was not until 1919 that a normal programme of matches was staged, by which time hundreds of men from the Monmouthshire Valleys had given their lives to King and Country.

Charles Gomery: Lest We Forget

One of the Blaina men to be killed in the Great War was Charles Gomery, who had enlisted in 1914 with the 6th Battalion of the King's Shropshire Light Infantry shortly before the birth of his fourth child. By the time Reginald was born, Sgt. Major Gomery had completed his basic training at Blackdown Camp before in April 1915 heading to Larkhill on Salisbury Plain for a final round of intensive training. In mid-July the battalion went by train to the Kent coast where they subsequently completed a rough crossing to Boulogne, before arriving at 3 a.m. in torrential rain at Osterhove Rest Camp. After some sustenance from the Salvation Army, the Battalion marched over cobbled roads and through thick mud to Borre, where they were then introduced to life in the trenches by the West Yorkshire Regiment.

Charles and the rest of the platoon then took part in preparations for what became known as the Battle of Loos. Tragically, he was one of four officers and 59 other ranks from the Battalion to be killed during the bloody battle, with Charles dying on October 2nd, 1915 at the age of just 41 from wounds received during a skirmish caused by a sudden German counter-attack. News of his death duly reached Blaina where his wife Mary was left to bring up alone the four young Gomerys. Like the thousands of other war widows the next few years were very tough for the family, but thankfully John, who had been barely five years old when his father was killed, gave her plenty to smile about as he played a leading role with the town club during the inter-war period.

The site where Bourneville CC are believed to have played before the Great War, with matches taking place in the field where the industrial unit now stands. The team was composed largely of workers from the South Griffin Mine and Roseheyworth

5
JOINING THE SOUTH WALES CRICKET ASSOCIATION

Continuing to raise the standard was uppermost in people's minds as cricket resumed after five bloody years in 1919, with schemes being introduced to further improve the game at both regional and local in South Wales.

As far as regional cricket was concerned, the Great War had temporarily extinguished Glamorgan's attempts at securing first-class status. After their success in the Minor County Championship, the county's officials began a fund-raising campaign, but a trade slump followed by uncertainty over the position in Europe halted their efforts. When club cricket resumed in 1919, attempts were made again by officials from the leading clubs to further raise standards by forming a League embracing the leading clubs in Monmouthshire, Glamorgan, Carmarthenshire and Pembrokeshire.

They had the ready support of the Glamorgan officials who believed that such a competitive structure was imperative to their success, allowing them to draw upon the cream of homegrown talent in the area, much in the way that the highly competitive Yorkshire and Lancashire Leagues had provided for many years a welter of talent for these northern counties. But no agreement was reached as the Glamorgan officials began planning their campaign for elevation into the County Championship and 1919 therefore witnessed the resumption of the usual round of friendlies and small local leagues.

The Blaina and Nantyglo area did however witness one important change as, through the initiative of Evan Watkins, an inter-colliery competition was instigated, starting in 1919. Watkins was now the manager of the South Griffin Pit and knew from his many years of working with the colliery staff that there were many people who would readily take part in such a competition, as well as the boost to the companies concerned from having a Cup competition. Indeed, the following eleven colliery teams participated in the inaugural year – Number 3 Griffin, Coalbrookvale, Stone's Pit B, Lower Deep, Rose Heyworth, Number 2 Griffin, Stone's Pit A, Lower Deep B, Hewwaun, North Slope and Lower Deep A – with the latter winning the Cup.

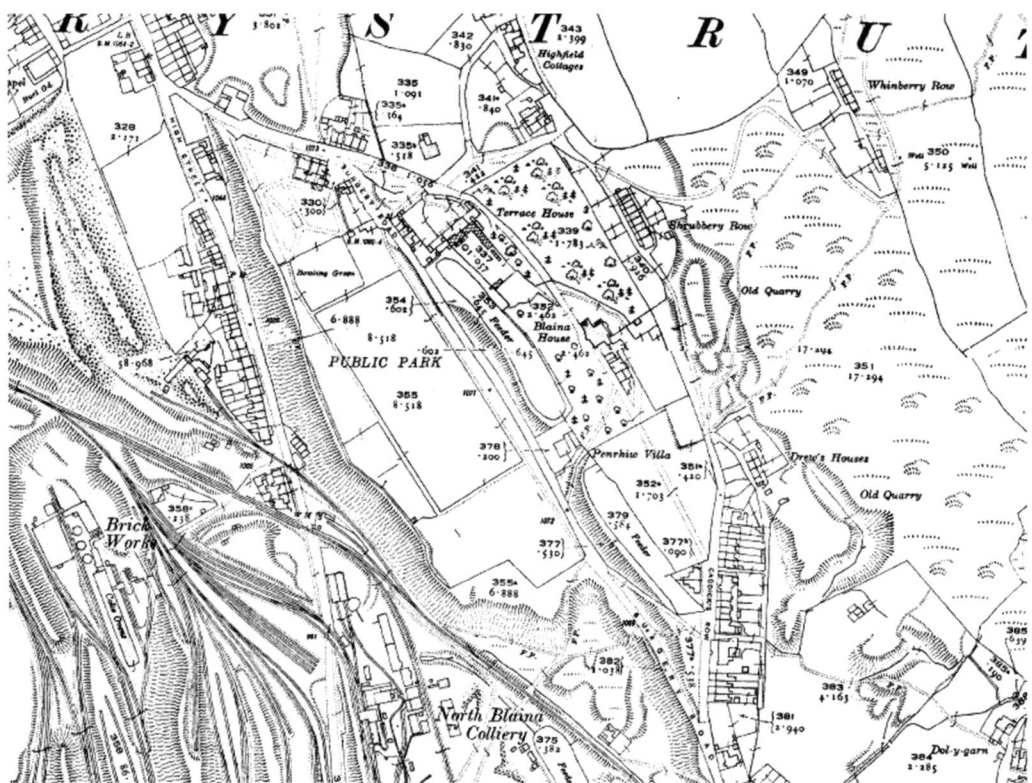

An Ordnance Survey map of the Blaina area from 1919

Watkins was also appointed captain of the Blaina side, and he celebrated his elevation with a fine century against Abertillery at Central Park. 1919 proved to be another successful year for the town club as they defeated Hereford City and Abergavenny, besides recording home and away victories against Crickhowell. As well as having their captain in prime form with the bat, Blaina could also call upon their experienced bowlers Vaughan Chaffey and Ivor Jones during the years immediately after the Great War. The pair continued their successful combination for several seasons, with Jones taking seven wickets against Abercarn in 1920, whilst Chaffey did the same against Dowlais the following year as he ended up with a haul of 61 wickets at just 10 runs apiece.

1921 also saw Watkins post another century against Abertillery, with the club's captain making an assured 113 at Central Park, with his fine form for Blaina leading to a recall to the Monmouthshire side for their Minor County Championship match against Devon at Abercarn. It wasn't altogether a happy return to county action as Watkins bagged a pair. Nevertheless, he remained

JOINING THE SOUTH WALES CRICKET ASSOCIATION

in good form for Blaina and the following year he added another hundred to his tally posting 104 in the match with Garndiffaith. Indeed, 1922 was a memorable year for Watkins as he was appointed General Manager of the Coalbrookvale colliery which was run by Sylvanus Jones and Company with a workforce totalling 250 men.

1922 however was a less happy year for the Blaina club as they encountered several financial problems. Watkins even dipped into his pocket and generously helped out the Club himself. Other local teams also encountered some financial problems and, at the end of the season, the town club merged with the Garn Primitive Methodist club, allowing them to field a third side in 1923. Another forward move also took place at the end of the 1923 season as the Blaina committee agreed to raise subscriptions in order that a groundsman could be appointed to maintain the good standard of the Central Park square.

Several new faces emerged during the 1920s with Joe Dally developing into a high quality seam bowler taking 7/39 in the narrow two-wicket victory over Abertillery in 1924, whilst the following year he took 6/22 against Ebbw

Blaina CC in the early 1920s

Joe Dally and his wife

Vale and 6/29 against both Tredegar and Newport 2nd XI. Tim Williams, or T.T. as he preferred, also came to prominence and deservedly was regarded as one of the fastest bowlers in the Monmouthshire Valleys. Tim was the younger brother of Jack Williams, the Welsh rugby international, and his cricketing career had started with the Salem Church side for whom he made his first appearance in May 1909. From here it was swiftly on to the Blaina United team and, after some highly promising performances, the young tearaway – who later became Headmaster of Garnfach School – joined the town club.

Either side of the Great War, Tim also showed his proficiency with the bat making 79 against Abertillery in 1913 and then 84 against Crickhowell in

1919, but it was during the 1920s that the seamer hit the headlines, taking 7/7 against Beaufort in 1923, followed later in the year by 6/8 against Dowlais. In 1925 he took 7/27 against Newport YMCA before recording the truly astonishing figures of 10/8 and 9/3 in two games against Nantyglo West. In the former match the Nantyglo side were dismissed for just 8 and Tim was subsequently presented with the match ball in recognition of his outstanding efforts. The county selectors were also impressed by his achievements, and in 1926 he made his debut for Monmouthshire in the Minor County Championship against Oxfordshire. Later in the season, he took 8/36 against Gowerton, before the next year taking 7/18 against Cardiff and causing mayhem amongst the ranks of what was regarded at the time as one of the best batting line-ups in the Association.

Tim Williams demonstrating his bowling action in 1925

Memorable Matches by Darryl Davies

Number 2 – All ten for T.T.

There have been no better playing years than Blaina's in 1925 and 1926, when the Club benefitted from the steady building and astute leadership overseen by Evan Watkins. One of the jewels in the crown of the Blaina club was Tim Williams who on June 6th, 1925 took 10/8 against Nantyglo.

Nantyglo

A Williams	c Parry	b Williams	0
A Phillips	c Tovey	b Williams	0
W Davies		b Williams	12
Watt Davies		b Williams	0
TJ Havard		b Williams	2
Phil Davies	c Dally	b Williams	12
T Williams		b Williams	3
G Powell		b Williams	0
I Jones		b Williams	1
F Thomas	not out		0
W Denning		b Williams	0
Extras			1
Total			31

Williams' bowling was a major factor behind Blaina's success in this golden era. He was also groomed by Evan Watkins as a future captain of the club, but this never occurred as a serious illness in 1928 curtailed his career, and despite some occasional appearances, he was never the same player. It is no coincidence that without Tim's bowling, Blaina found life very tough against the premier clubs of South Wales. His haul of 101 wickets – at just 7 runs apiece – in 1926 is one of only two instances of a hundred wickets in a season, whilst his figures of 10/8 remain the best-ever in Blaina's history.

Behind the stumps Alf Williams showed immense promise as a wicket-keeper, but his career with the Blaina club ended in 1923 when he emigrated to the United States. On the batting front, Len Chaffey, the younger brother of Vaughan, brothers Will and David Prout, plus Redvers Jeffreys all played useful innings as the next generation of Blaina cut their teeth under the wise

JOINING THE SOUTH WALES CRICKET ASSOCIATION

The match balls presented to Tim Williams after his record-breaking bowling feat in 1925

captaincy of Evan Watkins, who also formed a decent opening partnership with "Harry Jack" Hale with the pair sharing an unbroken opening stand of 123 against Newport 2nd XI in 1925.

Cricket was clearly on the up in the Blaina area, with the gates in 1925 double the amount they had been in previous summers. The Blaina 2nd XI were enjoying success under the captaincy of Percy Meyrick, whilst the colliery competition continued to be a great success. Indeed, there was sufficient interest in the game for the District Council to provide an auxillary series of wickets on the rugby ground besides installing a set of nets at Central Park. Evan Watkins also used his business contacts to secure donations from several colliery owners including Percy Hann, whilst Captain Evan Silk, the headmaster of Hafod-y-Ddol School also generously dipped into his pockets to swell the club's coffers.

1925 was a landmark season for both the Blaina club, and also for cricket in general across South Wales, as discussions resumed about creating a regional League, embracing the leading clubs from across Glamorgan, Monmouthshire and Carmarthenshire. Having such a system was imperative to the future of

Glamorgan CCC who had enjoyed a torrid team following their elevation into the County Championship in 1921. The euphoria of their elevation and their victory over Sussex in their inaugural first-class match quickly evaporated as the county club suffered a string of heavy defeats. Hiring professionals from other counties proved to be a false economy as many proved to be past their best, and the ambitious county officials realised that if the club was going to survive in the first-class world, they would need to foster their homegrown,

In short, a South Wales league was badly needed and during 1925 county officials met with representatives from across the region to see whether something could be created. Back in 1921 a Glamorgan County Cricket League had been instigated, largely comprising teams from West Wales. The First Division of the new League included Briton Ferry Steel, Briton Ferry Town, Gowerton, Hill's Plymouth (Merthyr), Port Talbot, Neath and Swansea, but clubs in the south-east were reluctant to join with the influential Cardiff club not wanting to forego some of their friendlies with some of the leading clubs in the West Country. Consequently, the League was disbanded after just a year.

But the situation was very different in the mid 1920s with the representatives from the Cardiff club, who so enjoyed hosting county cricket at the Arms Park and having close links with the county club, realising that it was imperative for a league system to be introduced if Glamorgan CCC was going to survive. Discussions therefore progressed with the premier clubs with Cardiff agreeing to join Barry, Briton Ferry Town, Briton Ferry Steel, Gowerton, Llanelli, Neath, Newport and Swansea in Division One of the new South Wales and Monmouthshire League.

Over thirty other clubs – including Blaina – also agreed to take part in a second division which in order to keep travelling distances, and costs to a minimum, was split into three regional sub-divisions – Monmouthshire, East and Mid Glamorgan, plus West Glamorgan and Carmarthenshire. Evan Watkins was the prime mover behind Blaina's participation in the new League realising the massive benefits it would bring for the club and the local area. With the club's finances now in a far healthier state and a raft of talented young cricketers emerging, the committee agreed with Watkins' suggestion and at Blaina's AGM in October 1925 it was announced to great applause that Blaina would be participating in Division Two of the new League alongside Abertillery, Abercarn, Chepstow, Ebbw Vale, Panteg, Pontymister, Pontypool and Tredegar.

6
THE FIRST GOLDEN ERA

May 1926 saw the inaugural matches in the South Wales and Monmouthshire League. It also coincided with deteriorating labour relations which culminated in the General Strike which lasted for ten days from May 3rd. The region's railway network was just one aspect of normal life to be thrown turmoil and, with the strike coinciding with the start of the cricket season, Blaina could not take a chance that they could travel by train, and instead the town's cricketers were reliant on travelling in an open-air charabanc. The Trade Union Congress, who had called the Strike, had many fervent supporters in the town's cricket club, especially those closely linked to the coal trade where the proposed wage reduction for miners and worsening conditions had been at the root of the unrest.

On a broader scale, the General Strike sent the town into poverty, with just 800 or so men working in the local colliery, whilst both Brick Works closed. Several local companies went bankrupt, whilst massive charitable funds poured into the Nantyglo and Blaina area, with £5,000 from Bermondsey & Rotherhithe.

The worsening economic position meant that cricket was barely talked about as the Blaina cricketers travelled around in their newly-hired vehicle. However, on their return journey from Chepstow at the end of the month, the fourteen-seater charabanc crashed into a house in Pontypool. The driver – George Hiley – escaped unscathed as the vehicle careered into the ground floor of Machine House. Two of the party though were not so fortunate. Tom Gurney, a bank clerk from Brynmawr, and George Tovey, a collier from Blaina, both sustained injuries and were knocked unconscious. Both came round after medical treatment, but Gurney had head and thigh injuries, whilst Tovey broke a leg. It was not the start to the season everyone had wanted, but thankfully both men were restored to health and, whilst convalescing from their injuries, each were regularly present at Central Park to see their Blaina colleagues enjoy a superb run of form in the new competition.

The season had begun with a draw against Barry and a six-run defeat against Abercarn, but the latter match proved to be a rare reverse as Blaina won eight successive League matches and become runaway leaders of Division Two (East). Their purple patch began, quite fittingly at Central Park where

THE HISTORY OF BLAINA CRICKET CLUB

The Blaina 1st XI at Abergavenny in 1926, including in the back row Harry Jack Hale (first left), Redvers Jeffreys (second left), Percy Meyrick (third left) and Mr. James (umpire).
Middle row – Tim Williams (first left), Evan Watkins (fourth left) and Joe Dally (fifth left). The front row includes Margaret Watkins, the daughter of Evan (second left), plus his son Ieuan (third left)

Panteg were beaten by 49 runs, thanks to a gritty captain's knock from EW Watkins. It was the Blaina bowlers though who took centrestage for the next couple of months, especially TT Williams and Joe Dally. For the former, 1926 was a truly memorable summer as the Blaina vice-captain took an aggregate of 101 wickets at just 7.17 runs apiece from 370 overs, with his outstanding efforts earning him selection, alongside his captain, in the Monmouthshire side which met Oxfordshire in their Minor County Championship encounter at Ebbw Vale.

Williams was regarded as the fastest bowler in the county – a most fitting monicker after he smashed a stump in half at Central Park as he dismissed a hapless Chepstow batsman. His fearsome reputation grew week by week as he claimed seven wickets in the home victory against a powerful Newport side at Central Park, besides an outstanding 8/36 from 22 overs in the 50-run defeat of Gowerton in a friendly at Blaina as the Monmouthshire side beat one of the leading lights from the First Division. Add to this a haul of 7/20 at Abercarn, plus 6/12 and 6/38 in the two games against the crack Abertillery side, another six in the away match at Pontymister, and five wicket hauls in games versus Tredegar, Panteg and Aberaman

Joe Dally was also in decent form with the ball taking five wickets against Abercarn, Tredegar and Chepstow, whilst Ivor Cook took 6/23 in the match with Pontymister including a hat-trick. On the batting front, Watkins led by example and, besides engendering a fine team spirit, he showed his class with half-centuries against Abertillery and Gowerton. Other batsmen contributed useful innings as well with David Prout making 65 against Abertillery and an unbeaten 69 against Panteg. HJ ('Jack') Hale struck 70* against Newport, whilst Tom Gurney, thankfully restored to the side after the charabanc accident, also struck a half-century against Tredegar.

Blaina's success led to bumper crowds at Central Park with around 4,000 present at the end of June for the local derby with Abertillery, and over 5,000 people attending the friendly against Gowerton on August 7th. Indeed, the Western Mail's cricket correspondent had noted a few weeks before that "rarely a Saturday passes without fuel being added to the fire of enthusiasm in the Monmouthshire end of the League." Much to the satisfaction of the supporters who attended the league games across South Wales, a regulation was also introduced that a game would only end when the home captain felt that the crowd had had their monies worth. Hence, several of Blaina's games continued for the crowd's pleasure even when the side batting second had passed their opponents score, with EW Watkins keen that the folk who turned up to Central Park were suitably rewarded for their loyalty.

Indeed, Ernie Barber still remembers that Central Park was the place to be on a Saturday afternoon during the summers of the twenties. In an interview for the *Taking the Field* project, he recalled how "at ten years of age, I would walk from my home in West Side through the Beynon Colliery tip towards Central Park. I never paid the sixpence to go into the Park because I was small enough to hide under the railings and watch the play!"

Cricket fever spread like wildfire through the community during the course of the 1926 season, as talk about the success of the town club replaced in every bar and on every street corner of the town, the moans and groans about the General Strike or grumbles about the prospect of a drop in wages. There was no shortage of willing helpers at the ground and, with a plethora of new members, the fixture list for the 2nd XI swelled. Other cricket teams in the town saw an upswing in activity and interest, and catching the mood of the locals, the cricket committee of the Blaina club arranged a special match at Central Park against the local councillors.

Ernie Barber

From mid-June, Blaina had been top of the table, with the Western Mail's correspondent in early July remarking how "Blaina will take some shifting from first place in the eastern section." They duly remained in top spot and on the last Saturday in August, Watkins' side clinched the Division Two (East) title by defeating Ebbw Vale by three wickets at Central Park. A fortnight later, the team were presented with the trophy after their match against Newport at Central Park, with a celebratory dinner held after the contest at which there were a series of speeches and presentations to the key players, including TT Williams, Dally and EW Watkins.

Whilst it was all smiles at the end of the summer in Blaina, elsewhere in South Wales there were plenty of grim faces. During the winter months several of the clubs participating in the South Wales and Monmouthshire League were badly affected by combined effect of the downswing in the local economy and the knock-on effects of the General Strike. The mining communities in the Rhondda and Monmouthshire valleys were worst affected

THE FIRST GOLDEN ERA

and with little money to spend on sports facilities, several clubs withdrew from the Second Division, including Llantwit Fardre, Penygraig, Pontypool, Pontymister and Ynysybwl, whilst Pontypridd Rugby League Club resigned a few weeks into the new season. Blaina were not immune to these financial difficulties, with the club ending their "golden summer" of 1926 with a modest balance of just 3 pounds and 7 shillings. Like other clubs, they incurred a sizeable expenditure, totalling 233 pounds, 3 shillings and seven pence.

Nevertheless, Watkins and the rest of the committee were adamant that the modest financial position should not affect the fortunes of the 1st XI – quite the opposite, in fact, with the Club officials doing all that they could to enhance their standing with Blaina securing home and away friendlies with Cardiff – one of the premier clubs in South Wales – as well as hiring John Vincett, a 44 year-old all-rounder who had played for Sussex between 1907

The Blaina CC 1st XI of 1926: Back row – Gwilym James (umpire), Percy Meyrick, Frank Athrone, David Prout, Redvers Jeffreys, Harry Jack Hale, Joe Dally. In suit – Richard Wetherall. Front row – Len Prior, Tim Williams, Evan Watkins, Ivor Cook, George Tovey, Elvet Wetherall. The children in the front are Margaret and Ieuan, Evan Watkins' daughter and son

and 1919, besides appearing for Surrey in 1921. Vincett had also appeared in previous years for Abertillery and it was quite a coup for Blaina to secure his services – they came though at an additional cost with Watkins and the club's committee arranging a series of social functions specifically to raise sufficient cash to cover the costs of signing the former county cricketer.

Vincett proved to be a useful acquisition as Blaina – to the delight of EW Watkins – won promotion to the First Division of the League, as they retained their title. The professional produced some excellent all-round performances as his side spent much of the season in a dog-fight with Ebbw Vale at the top of the table. Vincett began in mid-May by taking 5/8 against Hill's Plymouth as the Merthyr side were bundled out for 39. This was followed by a return of 6/28 in the 81-run victory over Tredegar, and then figures of 5/20, plus a forthright innings of 71 as Brynmawr were defeated by 85 runs.

Later in the season, Vincett took 6/43 as Ebbw Vale were beaten by four wickets, but his efforts with the ball at Abertillery could not prevent Blaina from losing to their local rivals for the first time since 1921. Vincett claimed 4/34 but was stumped for just 16 as Blaina – in front of a crowd of 4,000 – lost by eight runs. But the professional rectified matters when Abertillery visited Central Park ten days later, taking 7/24 as Blaina won by 110 runs. It was a comprehensive victory and the visiting side from Abertillery, who had walked to Blaina, must have had plenty on their minds as they trudged back home, somewhat earlier than they had expected.

Vincett was not the only bowler to enjoy plenty of success in 1927 because TT Williams once again produced some destructive spells taking 5/17 against Hill's Plymouth, besides recording five-wicket hauls against Abertillery and Abercarn. However, his finest spell of the summer came in the friendly with Cardiff at Central Park as Williams took 7/18 against a side containing several Glamorgan players as the visitors went down to a seven wicket defeat, much to the delight of the Blaina side.

By the closing weeks of the season, Blaina and Ebbw Vale were still locked together at the top of the table, with the latter having a slender lead on win percentage, largely because Blaina had had more games interfered with by the weather. The two sides met in mid-August in a contest that was likely to determine the outcome of the title, but once again the weather intervened and prevented Blaina, who had won the earlier contest in July, from improving their win percentage and denting their opponent's superior record.

The following weekend, rain washed out the entire League programme and the season duly ended with Ebbw Vale winning the Division Two title with a win percentage of 86.36% compared with Blaina's 85.71%. But there was good news for the Blaina cricketers a few weeks after the season had ended as League officials confirmed that the First Division was being enlarged

THE FIRST GOLDEN ERA

A presentation to a delighted Evan Watkins at Central Park in 1926

in 1928, with Blaina and Hill's Plymouth being elevated to play alongside Cardiff, Llanelli, Gowerton, Swansea, Newport, Neath, Barry and both Briton Ferry Town and Steel in Division One for the following season.

Many fulsome tributes were duly paid to the Blaina side for their efforts and enthusiasm in securing a position alongside the region's crack sides with the correspondent of the South Wales Gazette saying "they have reached their present position by determination, hard spade work, and the wonderful incentive continually displayed by the little band of workers who have mothered the team from the days when games with Winchestown and Nantyglo were looked upon as titanic struggles."

1927 was also a hugely successful year for one of the town's junior sides as Claytown won the Western Valleys Junior League. 1927 was also a red-letter year for EW Watkins as he was appointed Manager of the Pandy Colliery in Penygraig but, despite his new position, Watkins remained loyal to the Blaina club and over the winter months oversaw the arrangements for 1928 and life in the First Division. One of the thorniest issues discussed was the question of hiring a professional the following summer. Vincett had performed with credit on the field, but the club had incurred an overall loss of £12 and for several weeks, the finance committee debated the question of hiring a professional for 1928. After his success during 1927, Vincett received several offers from other clubs, elsewhere in South Wales and in England, and given the uncertainty about his position at Blaina, Vincett accepted an offer from an English club and left the Monmouthshire town, but not before a special function on his behalf at which the all-rounder was presented with a specially inscribed umbrella – a rather novel present for someone who did not want it to rain during the summer months!

Negotiations began with other professionals, including George Lavis, the highly promising 20 year-old all-rounder who was on Glamorgan's books and who had been a rising star in Monmouthshire cricket for the past few seasons. It would have been a major coup for Blaina – with EW Watkins' financial assistance to have secured Lavis' services – but he secured a position with another club in Glamorgan. Blaina eventually agreed terms with J.H. ('Joe') Pope, an experienced left-handed all-rounder who had played

Blaina's prolific opening batsmen – Pope and Hale

in the Yorkshire and Lancashire Leagues, and in 1927 had assisted Barry. He proved to be a useful acquisition, amassing over 600 runs including a fine century against his former employers at Central Park as Blaina defeated Barry by 18 runs. His experience at the top of the order proved invaluable as the Blaina side found the step up to the First Division quite a challenging one.

The season began with defeats to Newport and Swansea and, after their modest start, few outside the Monmouthshire town fancied their chances when they travelled to Cardiff to meet the reigning champions. But Blaina duly won at the Arms Park by five wickets, with the Western Mail newspaper hailing their success with the headline "How the Mighty are Fallen – League Champions beaten by Babes!" The architects of Cardiff's demise were bowlers Tim Williams and Tommy Lloyd who shared eight wickets between them as Cardiff slumped to 75/9 before a plucky last wicket stand of 41 gave the city side a modicum of respectability. Pope then overcame a hamstring strain by making 79 to steer Blaina to a handsome victory.

They were swiftly brought back down to earth with draws against Hill's Plymouth and Ebbw Vale, followed by a mammoth 168-run defeat by Swansea and a six-wicket loss against Neath. TJ Lloyd then restored their fortunes by taking five wickets in each of the home and away victories over Abertillery, plus a superb haul of 7/26 as Briton Ferry Town were defeated by eight wickets. Lloyd went one better in the game against Briton Ferry Steel, claiming eight wickets in the contest but his outstanding efforts with the ball could not prevent Blaina from being beaten.

In August, Blaina forsook their home advantage with Cardiff to return to the Arms Park again, and once again, the Monmouthshire club recorded another dramatic victory. The home side batted first and declared on 222/8 with Jock Tait, the Glamorgan batsman, completing a fine 130 with a straight drive against Tim Williams shattering the stumps at the non-strikers end. He duly became the first batsman to score a century against Blaina and was presented with the ball after the innings.

His efforts seemingly had put his team in a commanding position, but the Blaina batsmen had other ideas, as Tim Williams was promoted to open. With judicious use of the long handle, he ignited the run-chase with a rapid half-century before Pope maintained the momentum with the middle order. After the professional was dismissed, Evan Watkins – quite fittingly – came in to steer his side home by four wickets and with just over ten minutes to spare, almost to the disbelief of the Cardiff side who a couple of hours before had felt as if they were in an impregnable situation.

This proved to be Blaina's final success of the summer as the season ended with defeats against Newport, Neath and Llanelli as the Monmouthshire side ended in the lower half of the table. Despite their lack of collective success,

Memorable Matches by Darryl Davies

Number 3 – Victory over Cardiff in 1928

The match against Cardiff in the South Wales and Monmouthshire League was the plum fixture of the season, and the Blaina cricketers headed south to the Welsh capital with a mix of trepidation and excitement at the prospect of playing on the Arms Park. Cardiff were at full strength, with all of their first six having county experience with Glamorgan, whilst their captain was Norman Riches – one of the leading amateurs in county cricket.

Things did not go Blaina's way at first as they lost the toss and were handicapped by the late arrival of Ivor Cook, their left-arm fast medium seamer. But in his absence, the visitors opened up with Tim Williams, plus Tommy Lloyd, the left-arm spinner who claimed the prized wicket of Riches who was caught by a delighted Evan Watkins. Blaina then lost two early wickets in reply, before Pope drove beautifully through the covers until he was unluckily run out, leaving Watkins and WH Jenkins to see Blaina to a famous victory.

Cardiff

FW Mathias	c Prior	b Williams	23
WJ Evans	c Jeffreys	b Lloyd	8
HG Symonds	c Sparkes	b Lloyd	6
JR Tait	c Prout	b Williams	11
NVH Riches	c Watkins	b Lloyd	4
HW Taylor	c Prout	b Lloyd	2
J Valentine	lbw	b Williams	0
GL Rattenbury		b Lloyd	12
O Walker	c Cook	b Lloyd	5
A Gibbs	not out		26
AN Morgan		b Cook	14
Extras			9
Total			**120**

Blaina

JH Pope	run out		79
HJ Hale	c Riches	b Morgan	2
R Jeffreys	c and	b Valentine	3
DT Prout		b Valentine	15

WH Sparkes	c Symonds	b Walker	28
EW Watkins	not out		13
WH Jenkins	not out		23
I Cook			
GH Prior			
TT Williams			
TJ Lloyd			
Extras			**3**
Total	(for five wickets)		**166**

there had been some personal highlights, especially the good form of Pope who readily accepted terms for 1929, mixing his duties with Blaina alongside acting as cricket coach at Cowbridge Grammar School. The decent form of batsman Will Jenkins had been rewarded with selection in the Monmouthshire side that played Devon in the Minor County Championship match at Ebbw Vale, whilst both David Prout and TT Williams were included in the county's squad which played a friendly with Gloucestershire at the Rodney Parade ground in Newport.

During the winter months, the Blaina officials further strengthened their squad by hiring a second professional – Harry Ford, a right-arm fast bowler who had been playing with the Hill's Plymouth side in Merthyr. But 1929 was a modest year for the club as they won just three of their 18 matches. A serious illness meant that TT Williams did not appear until early June and his end-of-season tally was considerably less than in previous summers. In his absence, both Ford and TJ Lloyd produced some decent spells, with both bowlers playing a leading role in the victories over Briton Ferry Town and Newport. Ford also claimed six wickets in the home defeat by Maesteg, as well as a waspish four-wicket spell in the narrow defeat against Newport.

On the batting front, the highlight of 1929 was a remarkable century by Dick Parry who feasted on the Barry attack, going from 50 to 103* in the space of just eleven minutes. Parry struck 25 in one over, followed by 21 in the next as he raced to his maiden League hundred with a volley of aggressive blows. Pope also completed assured half-centuries against Abertillery and Newport, but overall the Blaina batting was not as consistent as in previous years and overly relied on EW Watkins, who was by now very much in the veteran stage.

Watkins showed his class by making an unbeaten 74 against Cardiff, but for the visit to Maesteg, duties at the colliery delayed his departure and he

THE HISTORY OF BLAINA CRICKET CLUB

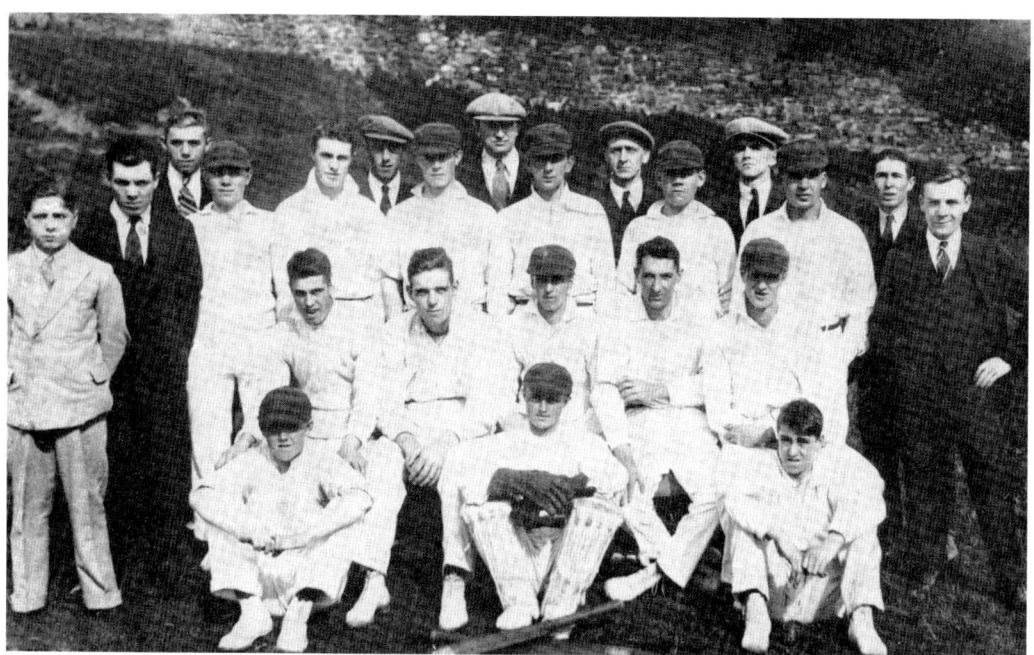

Waunmarsley CC in 1930

arrived too late to be included with Will Prout, the Blaina scorer, having to deputise instead. However, the nadir came in the game against Briton Ferry Steelworks as Blaina were dismissed for 34 with the West Glamorgan side comprehensively won by 207 runs. However, there was some young talent emerging with Elvet Wetherall, the son of the Blaina secretary, playing for Glamorgan Colts and Jim Austin winning selection in the Welsh Secretary Schools side that met the Glamorgan youngsters at the Arms Park.

7
THE BUBBLE BURSTS

With modest results, falling crowds and rising costs, many felt that Blaina's cricket bubble had burst by the end of the 1920s. For a start, the deficit at the end of the 1929 season meant that Blaina could not afford any professionals for the following season. They were also in arrears for their rent – at £7 per annum – of Central Park, but the council agreed to waive the debts, although some councillors did not agree with Blaina being treated more favourably than other clubs, especially when Abertillery were paying £25 each year for the use of their ground. EW Watkins also came to the club's aid once again, not claiming expenses when attending League meetings in Bridgend and helping to cover other small costs.

Other clubs were in a similarly poor financial situation but there were other issues as well, as in December 1929, Cardiff withdrew from the competition, upset at the levels of bad feeling and gamesmanship that were creeping into the matches, preferring instead the more pleasant and less antagonistic atmosphere of friendly matches. Indeed, there had been several cases of crowd trouble, with the worst being at Stradey Park in a top-of-the-table clash between Llanelly and Briton Ferry Steel. The barracking and general disturbances reached such a level that the umpires took the players off the pitch, and the game only resumed after both captains had gone into the crowd and spoken to the rival factions, pleading for peace and quiet.

Games at Central Park had been intensely played, but there were only isolated cases of bad sportsmanship or Blaina players questioning the decisions made by visiting umpires. The Monmouthshire side were not regarded as the chief culprits and, whilst their local derbies with Abertillery were keenly fought, it was extremely rare for a Blaina player to step over the line in terms of gamesmanship, whilst umpires Sam Bridgeman, Alf Hughes and Gwilym Jones rarely reported any incidents of bad behaviour.

1930 proved to be another poor year for the Blaina club, who finished bottom of the Division One table, with their sole victory coming against local rivals Abertillery who they dismissed for 50 thanks to 6/29 from Glyn Garrett. Both of their matches against Llanelli resulted in heavy defeats – the first match by 163 runs with Dick Butler, the Carmarthenshire club's wily professional taking six wickets after Jack Evans had posted a high-class 83. The

THE HISTORY OF BLAINA CRICKET CLUB

A modern-day view of Nantyglo and Winchestown, including the Nantyglo RFC ground. The rugby pitch was used by various local teams, including church teams, during the inter-war era

Winchestown CC in the 1930s

return game saw Evans make 98, but Butler was almost unplayable again, taking 7/18 as Blaina were dismissed for 43. EW Watkins top scored with 22 – as often in 1930 batting well down the order – to become one of only two batsmen to make double figures.

But even worse happened in the two games with Neath as none of the Blaina batsmen reached double figures in either game. At The Gnoll, Blaina were skittled out for 29, after TJ Lloyd had taken 8/46, whilst at Central Park, Bill Thomas took 6/13 including a hat-trick as the Monmouthshire side were bundled out for just 34. As well as these heavy reversals, there were several narrow defeats as well, with the matches against Ebbw Vale ending in one-wicket and two-wicket defeats. The former saw Ebbw Vale, chasing 145, collapse to 69/8 before their number eight batsman struck an unbeaten 61 to see Ebbw Vale home.

The modest form meant that the Club ended the year £62 in debt, and in the Spring of 1931 the council adopted a harder stance over the rent for Central Park, telling the Club to pay the arrears of £2 and 10 shillings after their first home game. As the season progressed, the poor financial situation meant that the club found it difficult to honour several away fixtures, with several 2nd XI matches being cancelled.

The lack of cash also meant that Blaina could not afford a professional, although it was hoped that John Vincett would turn out as an amateur in the second half of the summer. This failed to materialise, as Blaina lurched from defeat to defeat, failing to win a game throughout 1931 and ended bottom of the first Division table. The only crumb of comfort was the emergence of several young players, including Tom Collins, a pupil at Taunton School, who made 43 batting at number ten against Newport to help Blaina to a draw in the game at Central Park. Norman Bainton, a pupil at Hafod-y-Ddol School, also scored an unbeaten 75 batting at number four in the draw with Abertillery and was appointed captain of the Monmouthshire Secondary School side for their fixture against the Glamorgan Colts.

1931 also proved to be EW Watkins' final year in charge of the 1st XI. At the end of the summer he regrettably handed in his resignation, with WH Jenkins – a teacher at Nantyglo Elementary School and a former three-quarter with the Monmouthshire rugby side – taking over as captain, with Elvet Weatherall being appointed his vice-captain. However, there were doubts over whether the team could continue in the League and on March 4th, 1932 a meeting was convened at the King's Head Hotel to discuss ways of ensuring that the forthcoming fixtures could be met. At the gathering club officials outlined how £35 needed to be raised and, within a short space of time, fund-raising concerts by the Berea Dramatic Society and the local Operatic Society were successfully staged to raise much of the badly-needed funds. Later in the summer, a supporter's club was also formed to specifically plan regular fund-raising events during the winter months, with their plans including an Eisteddfod at the Church Institute.

With the funds coming in, things seemed to be looking up for the Blaina team, and there was further good news when the club acquired the services, as an amateur, of JM Lindsley, a useful all-rounder from Yorkshire who had plenty of experience in the Yorkshire Leagues and had claimed 90 wickets for Middlesbrough in 1931. But their new signing dislocated his right shoulder whilst practising ahead of the opening League match on Whit Tuesday against Neath at The Gnoll. However, his injury seemed to galvanise the Blaina team as they surprised their hosts with a narrow victory as, after TJ Lloyd had claimed four wickets, Frank Athron held his nerve as wickets plummeted to Frank Ryan, the Glamorgan spinner, with the Blaina man seeing his side home by the slender margin of two wickets.

The following week the winning run was maintained as Brynmawr were defeated in a friendly but, once League matches were resumed, it was back to the pattern of the previous year with a series of draws and defeats. One of the heaviest defeats came at Ebbw Vale where Len Pitchford, the local professional who went on to play for Glamorgan in the mid 1930's, took 6/22 as Blaina were bundled out for 50 before posting an unbeaten hundred as the home captain opted to bat on and provide further entertainment for the decent-sized crowd. Besides the loss of several senior players, another factor behind Blaina's poor run of form was the lack of firepower in their bowling, with Lindsley never really recovering from his shoulder injury and proving to be more effective with the bat than with the ball.

The Influence of Capt. Silk

Over the years, many schoolteachers have played a major influence in the development of cricket, and young cricketers, in Blaina. Pre-eminent amongst these was Capt. Evan Silk, the energetic Headmaster of Hafod-y-ddol School in Nantyglo, and a President of the Blaina cricket club, who himself grown up in the town before attending Cambridge University and serving in the Great War.

Silk was the school's first Headmaster, with the premises opening in 1924, and through his influence, it had a profound effect on the educational life of the area. Without the paternalistic attitude of men such as Capt. Silk, it is doubtful whether the club would be in such a healthy state.

THE BUBBLE BURSTS

The first school had opened in Blaina during the 1830s, with parish records stating that "on May 20th 1836 it was resolved unanimously that when the Poor house (Waen Goch) already let for a school room is no longer wanted for that purpose it be considered as let to Russell and Brown for cottages at the rental of £30 per annum." Further establishments had opened by the middle of the 19th century, including Nantyglo Ironworks School, Blaina Ironworks School and Cwmcelyn School – erected by the Levick's at a cost of over £3,000 – together with five private academies.

But in all of these, the curriculum was chiefly confined to the so-called three R's – reading, writing and arithmetic. Games and physical education were added at a later date, although the logbook for Blaina British Infants School on 7th August, 1865 does refer to "a tea-party held in the cricket field."

The W.S.S.C.A. Team 1931 with Norman Bainton (centre, middle row)

But it was not all doom and gloom in 1932 because, like the previous summer, several youngsters continued to make healthy progress, especially Norman Bainton – another former pupil of Hafod-y-Ddol School. The first signs of Bainton's decent headway came with a well-composed innings against Hill's Plymouth and Gowerton with the schoolboy just failing the make the fifty mark on each occasion. These were followed with a quickfire 48 in a dramatic run chase against Abertillery, with the youngster showing great composure beyond his tender years to see Blaina home by three wickets.

A fortnight later, Bainton made his maiden League century, with a highly polished innings of 101*, full of flowing drives through mid-off and mid-on against a decent Newport attack. His efforts didn't see Blaina to a victory as the talented Newport top-order feasted on the valley bowlers as the town side reached their target of 208 for the loss of just one wicket. Bainton added another unbeaten hundred to his tally in the draw against Abertillery and, after impressing many of the county selectors, the 18 year-old was chosen in the Monmouthshire side which met Oxfordshire at Ebbw Vale. He didn't let his supporters down in the Minor County Championship encounter as he ended up as top-scorer in Monmouthshire's first innings total of 104, with the schoolboy making 48 having arrived at the crease at number four with just a handful of runs on the board and resisting the visiting bowlers until being the last man out as he was stumped advancing down the wicket looking to secure the boundary he needed for a half-century.

The Glamorgan talent scouts were also keeping an eye on the youngster's progress, but in the winter months, Bainton accepted a post with the Civil Service in Bristol and left South Wales. He agreed to return at weekends to play for Blaina, but he only appeared occasionally during the summer months and his loss was a massive blow – both for Blaina cricket and Glamorgan CCC. Later in 1933 another promising talent left the area, with Kenneth Davies, son of former captain TL Davies, graduating from Cambridge University and – like Bainton – moving to work in London for the BBC. Davies had shown signs of great promise with the bat in 1933, with the student making 103 against Brynmawr, 71 against Hill's Plymouth and 68 against Pontardawe. He continued to play for a while after coming down from Peterhouse in mid July, but his talents as a batsman were lost by the end of the summer.

In all, Blaina won just a couple of League matches in 1933 beating Pontardawe by three wickets and Hill's Plymouth by just four runs in a keenly fought contest. Once again, the enthusiastic Blaina cricketers struggled against the premier sides in the region although John Gomery and John Moody showed promise with the bat, whilst Joe Dally and George Tovey proved to be useful bowlers. But without a professional, Blaina found it hard to compete against the best clubs in the region, especially those who could afford to hire a county professional or

THE BUBBLE BURSTS

some of the aspiring talent. A case in point came in June when Blaina met Elba but the First Division's new boys proved to be far too strong, winning by seven wickets with opening batsman David Blackmore, who subsequently played for Glamorgan, making a fine half-century. A fortnight later, Evan James – another county player – took 8/34 as Briton Ferry Town routed Blaina by nine wickets, whilst later in the season, Blaina lost to Ebbw Vale by seven wickets as, for the second year in succession, Len Pitchford struck an unbeaten hundred.

It came as no surprise therefore that, at the end of the 1933 season, Blaina decided to withdraw from the League. The year before Newport had also opted out of the competition, as like Blaina, they found it increasingly expensive to continually head down to West Glamorgan and Carmarthenshire for their matches. Moreover, one of the requirements for being a Division One club was having decent facilities, with well-maintained sightscreens and scoreboards, plus a decent wicket. In 1933, the local council kindly dropped the rent for Central Park down to four guineas, and also covered the costs of improving the wicket with marl, but even so, the Blaina Club still had sizeable travelling costs as well as an overall deficit. With a young side taking to the field without a professional, often against another team with two or three paid players, it was clear that Blaina were on a hiding to nothing by playing in the South Wales and Monmouthshire League, and at the end of the summer they copied Newport's example by withdrawing from the competition.

8
BODYLINE AT BLAINA!

The winter of 1932/33 will forever be remembered as the time when cricket took over the front pages of the national newspapers with coverage of the England touring team, under Douglas Jardine, against Australia and the use of fast leg-theory by the tourist's in a bid to combat the batting genius of Don Bradman and others in the Australian line-up. It led to bitter exchanges on the field, and even to tersely worded statements being sent between the country's politicians, with cricketers resting back home in England and Wales being sharply divided over the fairness of what became known as Bodyline bowling.

Like most things in cricket, what happens in the national team, soon disseminates down to the county sides, with several professionals using the tactic in 1933, including Bill Bowes of Yorkshire who unfortunately injured Glamorgan's Johnnie Clay with a sharply rising ball. It was not long before it was used in club cricket and during 1934 Rumsey James, the young Blaina fast bowler adopted similar tactics in Blaina's match against Abertillery. With the latter still in the South Wales League, the contest was a friendly, but there was nothing friendly about the way James exploited a slightly damp surface, making the ball rise up sharply off a length up into the body of the Abertillery batsmen.

John Moody, the Blaina captain also employed a ring of close catchers as James scythed his way through the Abertillery line-up. In all, he took seven wickets but, according to the correspondent in the South Wales Gazette, only one of the wicket-taking balls would have struck the stumps. A few ribald comments were exchanged around the boundary ropes about the merits and ethics of the Blaina tactics but, at the end of the day, Abertillery got home with two wickets to spare. Unlike the games in Australia when telegrams had been exchanged between politicians, matters between Blaina and their local rivals did not unduly escalate, with many people also suggesting that it was youthful exuberance rather than malice which had prompted James to employ such tactics. But Moody had also been compliant in the events, and had not told his young bowler to stop bowling leg-theory. At the end of the season, Moody was not re-appointed as captain, and one can only speculate whether EW Watkins – the eminence grise of Blaina cricket and a good churchgoing fellow – had been embarrassed by his choice of tactics.

Fortunately, the return fixture later in the 1934 season against Abertillery was less feisty but, even so, it still saw a notable feat by a young Blaina bowler with Ron Evans taking 10/34 in the drawn fixture. Evans was yet another product of Nantyglo Secondary School who had moved away to complete his studies and to find work, but he had returned to his family's home in August and helped out the Blaina club whilst on holiday. This time, it was all for the right reasons that plenty of column inches in the South Wales Gazette were given to a description of the Blaina bowling, with Evans being presented with the ball after the game in recognition of his outstanding feat.

This was the undoubted highlight of the 1934 summer – a season which saw Blaina complete a less taxing fixture list compared with previous years, playing the likes of Llanhilleth, Panteg, Abercarn, Chepstow, Pontypridd and Cross Keys instead of the crack sides in the region. But, after the excitement and experience of playing against the cream of the amateur and professional talent in South Wales, there was an inevitable low key air to many of the Blaina fixtures. The flip side of this was that several aspiring young players followed the example of Elvet Wetherall, who had joined Abertillery over the winter months, by moving to play for other clubs in the hope of playing at a higher standard.

The Blaina Miners Fete on Central Park in 1932

One of these was Gomer Evans, a product of Nantyglo Wesleyans CC and a more than useful rugby player with the Nantyglo All Blacks. At the age of fifteen, Evans had made 107 for Nantyglo Wesleyans against Brynmawr Church School, and for a short while he had played for Blaina. However, Evans was very ambitious and he accepted an offer to play for Brynmawr. His all-round talents soon attracted the attention of Bill Hitch, the newly appointed coach of Glamorgan, and the former Surrey and England bowler invited Evans to play for the Glamorgan Colts, before making his debut for Glamorgan 2nd XI against Dorset in the Minor County Championship contest at Ebbw Vale in 1935.

Monmouthshire CCC

Blaina were not alone in facing financial problems in the early 1930s. In fact, Monmouthshire CCC wound up their activities with the Gwent side failing to achieve their dream of first-class status.

Formed in 1892, the Monmouthshire County Cricket Association initially organised matches against neighbouring Welsh and English counties. It's leading figure was Fred Phillips – a member of the well-known brewing family from Newport and captain of the town's club.

Their activities expanded in 1901 as Monmouthshire joined the Minor County Championship, with hopes of one day joining the first-class ranks. However, by the early 1930s, the Monmouthshire club was beset with financial problems and they merged with Glamorgan with the latter's 2nd XI taking the Gwent teams place in the Minor County competition. Promising youngsters from Monmouthshire, such as Blaina's Gomer Evans, therefore got a chance to play for the county's Colts and 2nd XI.

Gomer Evans

The following year, Evans accepted a post with Surrey County Council in Banstead, and the promising youngster duly plied his trade with great success in the Club Cricket Conference, leaving Blaina officials rueing the fact that so many good players were leaving the district. Another notable departee had been David Prout who was promoted to the post of Assistant Superintendant with the Refuge Assurance Company in Cardiff. The loss of the experienced batsman, and noted rugby referee, was a another blow for the Blaina club, but tragically an even larger one hit the Prout family in 1937 when David died prematurely at the age of just 39.

There were many other worries though for the Club in the mid-1930s, not least the way that the local economy had been in a constant downward spiral for several years. The 1920s had experienced a phase of colliery closures as the owners desperately tried to maintain profit margins in the wake of reduced demand and rising costs. Output in the South Wales coalfield as a whole plunged from 57 million tonnes in 1913 to 48 million in 1929 and then to 35 million by 1935.

During the 1920s the problems began with a phase of sporadic closures as men were hired and subsequently fired as the mines opened and closed. A further problem was that the output from Ebbw Vale steelworks also declined, and the net result was that by the start of the decade known as "The Hungry Thirties" only eight collieries remained in Nantyglo and

The Lower Deep Mine

The South Griffin Mine

Blaina – Coalbrookvale, Deep Coal Pit, North Blaina, Beynons, Lower Deep Coal Pit, West Blaina Red Ash, Henwaun and South Griffin.

For many communities in the Monmouthshire valleys where life revolved around the pit, these closures set in train a host of social problems. With unemployment in Blaina estimated at around 60% by 1933, slum housing and malnourishment were commonplace. Despite the donation of £1,270 from Willesden in 1930, and £20,000 from the Mansion House Fund poverty was now a constant companion, and as the towns of Blaina and Nantyglo became more bedraggled and run-down, local surgeons became unwilling to operate on the physically weak patients.

Despite these problems of extreme poverty and deprivation, this was a period of little state intervention to diminish the problems caused by unemployment, and the policies implemented at the time by the government led to sizeable local unrest and riots in Blaina in March 1935. At the root of the problem was the Means Test introduced by the government, to assess the needs of unemployed men and their families. Public Assistance Committees had been created to assess all income, savings and possessions of the claimant, but the programme was run unevenly and, at a time when many felt that the government should be making more funds available to reduce the appalling problems caused by unemployment, many people resented the intrusion into their personal life and the questions which the committees asked.

BODYLINE AT BLAINA!

Beynons Colliery

Henwaun Pit

A National Unemployed Workers Movement had been formed and it was estimated that around 60% of unemployed men in Blaina belonged to the organisation. In January 1935 a protest had taken place at Nantyglo about the Means Test and possible further reductions in unemployment assistance, with over 2,000 people attending the meeting, including many women carrying small children and babies whilst in February a massive demonstration was also held in Abertillery Park. Some viewed these activities and meetings as communist activity, but with the problems caused by poverty and unemployment ever rising, feelings were running high and, when in March 1935 a local Blaina councillor was refused an interview with the Public Assistance Committee to propose solutions to the scheme, a protest march was planned for later in the month.

Initially, it was agreed that the march could take place with everyone gathering on Central Park and a group of a dozen marchers being then escorted by the police to the Public Assistance Committee's offices for a meeting. However, a U-turn then took place with the police banning the march and not agreeing to escort the deputation to the offices. The march duly took place on March 21st 1935 with clashes between an estimated 5,000 unemployed people and the police. Over two dozen officers were injured as bitter fighting broke out and in the following days, the leaders of the march were arrested, and in all, 18 men were charged with assault. Additional police were deployed to the Monmouthshire town, as fears grew about the possibility of further riots, but fortunately no more civil unrest took place.

9
THE CRICKETERS GO TO WAR

For the second time in their history, Blaina's cricketers gathered for the start of a new season against a backdrop of civil unrest and riots, with the players gathering at Central Park in April 1935, a month or so after the sports ground had been the unwitting venue for some of the protests against the Means Test and Public Assistance Committee. The situation was certainly not as tense when the town's cricketers gathered for their first outdoor practice of the summer, but the talk in the pavilion was still about the lack of work and the spin-offs caused by the mass unemployment. The situation was sufficiently grim for John Dakers to resign as General Manager of the Lancaster Colliery and, with the prospect of no new work coming into the area, those people who could afford to leave left with their families seeking a fresh start elsewhere.

The major impact on the cricket club was a dramatic drop in membership by the start of the 1935 season. With the on-going financial problems, several fixtures had to be curtailed, and economy measures were put in place, including reduced membership fees, so that every penny could be wisely spent. Despite this unhappy backdrop, 1935 witnessed some decent performances, especially by the bowlers, with Rumsey James taking 5/11 against Llanhilleth in 1935 as Blaina won by 156 runs. He also took 5/41 in the draw with Abertillery – this time not employing Bodyline tactics and bowling to a much fuller length. His younger brother Phil also made headway as a bowler, capitalising on his tutelage at Hafod-y-ddol School under the watchful eye of Captain Silk as well as some useful tips from his elder brother. James junior claimed five wickets in the victory against Llanhilleth in 1936, and also played some useful innings in the middle order but, like the rest of the Blaina side in 1936, he was frustrated by the poor weather and the loss of many games to heavy rain which further blighted the cricket season.

The loss of so many fixtures to the weather in 1936, as well as the worsening economic situation, only added to the Blaina's club deficit. By 1936 it was estimated that around 7,000 people had left the area, and in November 1936 a group of 40 unemployed men from Brynmawr, Nantyglo and Blaina joined a group of five hundred protesters from South Wales who went to London to peacefully protest about the appalling situation brought about

Central Park in 1940

by several years without work. The following month, Thomas Johnston – a Labour MP – also tabled a question in Parliament asking what could be done to improve the welfare of pupils at the schools in Blaina, where the Headmasters had reported around half of the children were underfed and undersized, besides being poorly shod and clothed.

With the financial situation not improving, the Blaina club cancelled several fixtures during 1937 and it was only after a small gift from EW Watkins that other games towards the end of the season could take place. After a couple of years of quite severe austerity measures, and reduced membership fees, some officials started to doubt if the Club could continue, especially when there were still around 2,000 unemployed men in the town. At the end of the season, the Club officials attempted to secure fixtures for the following summer, as well as arranging the use of Central Park, but the parlous financial situation meant that the Club couldn't make any financial guarantees, not even to the Council over the use of the Park. Things remained grim early in the New Year and, with the position no better in the Spring, a public meeting was consequently held at the Reading Institute on April 22nd to discuss whether or not the Club could continue.

After considerable discussion, it was decided to arrange fixtures for May 1938 and to review the position after the first month of the season. A further round of cost-saving measures were introduced and, realising that the future of the club lay in the balance, everyone pulled together to ensure that further fixtures could be honoured – even to the extent that Club members made sandwiches and cakes themselves for the visitors and did not charge the Club a penny.

With the situation having not deteriorated drastically by the end of May, the Blaina officials were able to arrange games for the rest of the summer and, almost by means of celebrating the situation, Rumsey James took 6/15 against Blaenavon Forgeside by 104 runs. John Gomery and George Tovey were also in decent form with the ball later in the summer, with each claiming four scalps in the five-wicket victory against Abertillery. However, their finest hour came against St. Athan as the village side were dismissed for 25 with Gomery taking 4/1 and Tovey 4/9.

But some of the smiles became less broad on the face of the Blaina cricketers as, towards the end of 1938, Rumsey James confirmed that he too was moving to a post in Surrey, and the early part of the 1939 season saw two of the area's finest young cricketers playing with credit for Banstead, as James and Gomer Evans hit the headlines with their opening partnerships. Fortunately, James returned to South Wales for a few weeks in August, allowing him to appear in the local derby against Abertillery. He duly celebrated his return by taking three wickets and hitting an unbeaten 64 as Blaina won by three wickets. The following week he also took 6/20 against Cyncoed as the Monmouthshire side defeated the club from Cardiff and, not to be outshone by his elder brother, Phil James also claimed 5/4 against Llanhilleth as Blaina won by 127 runs with their opponents dismissed for just 33.

However, by the time the James brothers were back in tandem for Blaina, far more weightier matters were occupying everyone's minds. Events on the world stage had steadily taken a turn for the worse and, with war clouds gathering over Europe in June and July, the Blaina cricketers were only too keen to take their minds off the ever-worsening situation by getting their whites on every Wednesday or Saturday afternoon.

With war being declared on Germany on September 3rd, 1939, and people signing on for King and Country, the last few matches of the summer were very tame affairs. Central Park was also used by the Armed Forces and, for the next six years, the cricketers from Blaina were involved fighting far greater battles on foreign soil. One can only wonder what was going through the mind of Jack Brookes as the Blaina cricketer headed across the English Channel in June 1944 to take part in the Normandy Invasion. No doubt, happy memories of playing cricket, and other sports, helped him and countless thousands of other men get through the long and grim days of the War.

John Gomery was another Blaina cricketer whose memories of sunny days at Central Park helped him get through some difficult times. John had been

Blaina's captain in 1938 and 1939, as well as being their Secretary between 1934 and 1938, before signing on as a gunner in the Royal Artillery shortly after War had been declared. Gomery was a Blaina man through and through, having been raised by his mother who had been widowed during 1915 when Charles Gomery was one of thousands of brave young men to fall in the Battle of Loos. From his early teens, John enjoyed playing cricket and rugby for the town club, and he passed on his love for ball games and team sports after completing his teacher training at Caerleon Training College, prior to starting as Blaina Central Boys School. His early years in education coincided with the Depression years, with boys aged 14–18 at the Central School earning their dole money by learning woodwork, metalwork and some basic English.

John Gomery, in his days as a Headmaster

In 1941 Gomery was posted to Malaya but was captured when Singapore fell in February 1942. He spent the next three years in captivity in a Japanese P.O.W. camp and worked on the Burma railway – the notorious railway of death for hundreds of Allied prisoners – and was amongst the lucky ones who were still alive at its completion in summer 1943. He was subsequently transferred to Ubon in Thailand, where he helped build aerodromes, before being liberated in 1945. The arrival of a letter at his family's home in Six Bells, Abertillery in early October was greeted with a heady mix of joy and sheer delight as for the first time in over two years there was confirmation that he was still alive, quashing fears that, like his father back in 1915, he might have given his life for King and Country.

However, John was suffering, like so many other POW's, from severe weight loss, malnutrition and dysentery. By the time he was discharged from the military in February 1946 he was in a more robust state, but he still had the dark and stark memories of life in captivity. John carried these mental scars for the rest of his life, at first only sharing them with close family members.

THE CRICKETERS GO TO WAR

> ### John Gomery's Reflections
>
> In March 1971 John Gomery reflected on the terrible days he suffered as a prisoner-of-war in the Far East in an interview with *The South Wales Argus*:
>
> "You had to get into a mental attitude of living day by day, of having no other life, so gradually you forget about home. The only thing to do was to accept the inevitable, and that type of mental attitude helped to save the people who got through it in some sort of sanity. It was as bad as it has been depicted by writers. But the compensation was that there is nothing like such an experience for character building. Having got through it, helped to give me a slant on life which helped, being in a position to understand real values."

The mental scars meant that John found it difficult at first to adjust back to civilian life and in 1946 he cut short his leave and took a teaching post at Park Terrace Junior School in Pontypool. His career duly blossomed and in 1953 he became headmaster of Garn-yr-Erw Junior Mixed School in Blaenavon. He subsequently held headships at Llanhilleth and Abertillery Boys, before in 1968 being appointed head of Cwmtillery Junior School, known to countless numbers of pupils as" the cock and chick". At all of these institutions, John brought warmth and good humour to the classroom, as well as ensuring that team games featured prominently on the school's curriculum – something that the area's sporting organisations were very grateful for as life started to get back to normal after the horrors of the War.

John Gomery in his military uniform

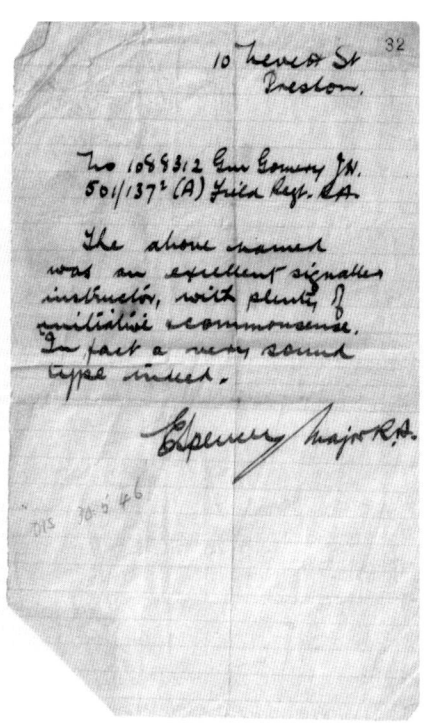

John Gomery's war letters

10
LEAGUES AND CHAMPIONSHIPS

For many years, there had been talk of a Monmouthshire League, with the leading clubs in the county all participating. Hastings Clay, the venerable patron of Chepstow CC and the father of Glamorgan's Johnnie Clay, had been an early proponent and his suggestion received support from many other officials during the 1930s, ironically after Monmouthshire had left the Minor County Championship in 1934 and merged with Glamorgan. In 1937 a further attempt had been made to form a Monmouthshire League, with Blaina swiftly indicating a willingness to take part. Officials from Beaufort, Brynmawr, Llanhilleth, Rogerstone, Pontymister and Abertillery were also keen to take part, although the officials of Newport showed indifference to the idea, preferring instead to play friendlies with clubs in the West of England, as well as in Glamorgan.

Nothing immediately came of the suggestion but, as far as Blaina were concerned, playing in any sort of League and making monetary commitments would have been pie in the sky given their poor financial position. But when cricketing activity resumed after the Second World War, the club's finances were healthier. There was also a feel-good factor permeating through the Monmouthshire valleys as life – whether it be domestic, industrial or sporting – gradually got back to normal. When the idea of a Monmouthshire League was put forward again in 1946, there was plenty of support, including from those in Blaina who had successfully staged a few wartime matches on Central Park to raise money for the War Effort as well as for the cricket club.

Another bonus was the fact that EW Watkins agreed to come out of retirement and lead the club and it was almost like 1926 all over again as the 64 year-old proudly led out the Blaina side as they met Abertillery in their inaugural Monmouthshire League match in May 1946. The veteran batted at number 11 and fielded at slip as the next generation of young cricketers did their best with bat and ball to re-establish the good name of Blaina CC. It greatly heartened him to see so many youngsters joining the club. There was further good news the following year when both Gomer Evans and Rumsey James returned to work in the district, with each re-joining the club which was now led by Rumsey's younger brother Phil who had taken over from the venerable Watkins.

Amongst those returning to action was Ron Smith, who had been a loyal member of the side in the 1930s, and he resumed in the Blaina side alongside a clutch of new faces, including Howard Knight. The only down side for the eager band of old and new cricketers was that the Monmouthshire League had been discontinued and throughout the summer a series of friendlies were staged. Several of the youngsters made headway, especially Mostyn Williams who took 6/15 in the draw away to Abertillery. In 1947 the visit of Abertillery to Central Park drew a bumper crowd. Many expected the two professionals to take centre stage – Cyril Smart, the former Glamorgan batsman, who was playing for Abertillery, and Blaina's George Oldham. But it was the legendary Blaina wicket-keeper, Bill Davies Colt, who stole the show with a superb century for the home side. Bill subsequently had trials with Glamorgan and subsequently gave loyal service to Blaina for the next decade, with his outstanding efforts being marked in 1956 with life membership of the club.

As the 1947 season progressed, the club's finances continued to improve and, when a Western Valleys Championship was suggested for 1948, Blaina expressed a keen interest to participate. With other leading clubs in the area also following their lead, plans were set in motion for 1948, with Blaina also starting a search for a suitable professional who could be hired to assist them in the new competition.

Their choice was George Oldham, who had been on Sussex's staff before the War but had not appeared in Championship cricket. Their new acquisition, however, made an immediate impact when the Western Valleys Championship began in May 1948, as Blaina – now under the captaincy of Gomer Evans – defeated Pontymister by 163 runs with Oldham claiming five wickets and Rumsey James three as their opponents were bundled out for 45.

This was the start of a purple patch which saw Blaina record a further five successive victories, starting with a 118-run defeat of Abertillery with Gomer Evans making 68 and Rumsey James claiming four wickets. The latter took a further four the following week as Pontymister were defeated by 167 runs, with Mostyn Williams displaying his batting credentials with a fiery half-century. Panteg were the next side to be beaten by Blaina as debutant Graham Lockstone took 7/24 on his first appearance.

The bowling of Mostyn Williams was a key factor in the next two victories as Girlings (Cwmbran) were beaten by 20 runs, with the bowler taking 7/18 after Gomer Evans had posted a solid fifty. The following week Williams took 5/24 as Brynmawr were defeated by six wickets as Blaina extended their lead at the top of the Championship table.

Indeed, cricket was at the forefront of sporting conversations throughout the area as, besides Blaina riding high in the local competition, Glamorgan were on top of the County Championship with Wilf Wooller's team pressing

LEAGUES AND CHAMPIONSHIPS

for their inaugural county title, and there was plenty of chatter about both teams securing their titles. A decent-sized crowd therefore were present for the local derby with Abertillery, but rain spoilt the contest shortly after the latter had declared as the match ended in a watery draw after Blaina had batted for just a couple of overs. But the following weekend, they swiftly returned to winning ways as Brynmawr were beaten by 22 runs with Lockstone, Williams and James sharing the wickets.

The August Bank Holiday saw the Blaina cricketers and their happy band of supporters visit Barry Island for a friendly against the local club. The match ended in a draw but, on their day out at the coastal resort, there was plenty of happy chatter about Glamorgan lifting the County Championship and Blaina winning the Western Valleys competition. Both happened as Wilf Wooller's team defeated Surrey at the Arms Park followed by Hampshire at Bournemouth, before Blaina finished the season with a comprehensive victory by 37 runs over Abertillery, with Mostyn Williams taking 4/22, before

Blaina CC players gather at Central Park for a match in the mid 1950s. Standing are Roy Dash, Bryn Wiltshire, Brian Jenkins, Mike Amos, Mel Gore, Eddie McDonald, Harry Niner, Jack Brookes and Gareth Saunders. The children sitting are Glyn Jenkins, Gareth James, unknown, unknown, Keith James, Ron Jones and another Gareth James

British Nylon Spinners (Pontypool) were dismissed for 28 as Gomer Evans' team became Western Valley Champions.

The good form of the Blaina side was continued the following summer, as 13 out of the 23 matches were won. Whilst opening batsman Jimmy James regularly gave the innings a decent start, it was Gomer Evans, Mostyn Williams and Rumsey James who all produced stellar performances in securing victories for the Blaina side. As in the previous summer, Evans led from the front with bat and ball, making 73 in the victory against Pontymister before taking 6/40. His best performance of the summer however came against Pontnewynydd where he made a fine 105 before claiming 7/44 as Blaina won by 116 runs.

James also gave a glimpse of his batting talents with a half-century against Llanhilleth, but his finest hours were with the ball as he claimed 5/5 in the victory against British Nylon Spinners (Pontypool) followed by 5/12 in the match against Cardiff 2nd XI. Mostyn Williams claimed 7/15 against British Nylon Spinners, and all after Blaina had been bustled out for 52 courtesy of a hat-trick by Charles Millman. But Williams also took 6/21 in the draw with Pontymister, before claiming 5/26 as Abertillery beaten by 153 runs.

The match with Girlings the following year saw Williams display his talents with the bat as he struck a quickfire 62* as Blaina posted 172/6 in just an hour and a half. 1950 also saw some standout performances from some new faces, with Glyn Harvey making 52 against Abertillery – a match at Central Park which also saw the wicket-keeper post a useful 44. With the ball, Graham Lockstone took 4/20 in the victory over Panteg by 80 runs, whilst Rex King claimed 4/39 in the thrashing of Abertillery by 173 runs. The latter match, though, also saw Gomer Evans take 5/19 and the Blaina captain really had a summer to savour in 1950. He began the summer by taking 7/38 in a four-run victory over Blaenavon before taking 3/12 in the victory over Abercarn, including the last two wickets with the final couple of balls of the thrilling contest. Evans also showed that he was not a spent force with the bat in the friendly with Cardiff, as he posted an accomplished half-century in the drawn contest.

Nevertheless, great excitement had been generated locally by the visit of the Glamorgan side, and dozens of local schoolboys swarmed around the pavilion with their autograph books looking to get the signature of England all-rounder Allan Watkins, plus other members of the Welsh county's 1948 Championship-winning team including Jim Pleass and Norman Hever, rising stars Bernard Hedges and Don Shepherd, county veteran Cyril Smart plus Lavis himself. But for one young Blaina boy, the next week ended tragically as the day after the visit by the Glamorgan side to Central Park, sixteen year-old David Edwin Jones of Glan Ebbw badly cut his right index finger whilst

LEAGUES AND CHAMPIONSHIPS

A Visit by Glamorgan

Gomer Evans was also instrumental in arranging a visit by the Glamorgan team on August 16th to Blaina for a match in aid of George Lavis' Testimonial Year. For several weeks before their visit, groundsman Ivor Williams spent extra hours carefully preparing the wicket for the match against the county professionals, whilst plans were put in place for a reception for Lavis and his colleagues before the match, plus a dance after the contest. The only thing, though, that the Blaina club could not control was the weather and sadly after the Glamorgan side had made 23/1, rain started to fall washing out the rest of the contest.

George Lavis

playing cricket with his friends. Despite treatment from local doctors, septicaemia set in and the youngster died five days later.

During the winter months, the Blaina Club also lost one of its leading lights with the death in 1951 of Dick Wetherall. He had been the Club's Secretary since the early 1920s and had witnessed their first Golden Era in the 1920s, their years in the South Wales and Monmouthshire League, plus the post-war resurgence. A close friend of Evan Watkins, Dick had worked at Beynons Colliery and North Blaina Pit, besides being the organist at Berea Congregational Church since his late teens. His funeral saw a massive turnout from the local community and his passing – at the age of 60 – marked the end of an era in Blaina cricket with a special plaque in his memory being unveiled at the ground the following Spring.

11
INTERNATIONAL CRICKET COMES TO BLAINA

Central Park was the venue in 1951 for festivities associated with the Festival of Britain as, like the rest of the country, the settlements in the Monmouthshire valleys took part in a series of community celebrations between May 26th and June 3rd, with a week of choral concerts, operatic renditions, community hymn singing, theatrical performances and an Eisteddfod on the closing night. From a cricketing point of view, matches were staged against local rivals at the start and the end of the week, but a couple of weeks later there was little to celebrate as Blaina's impressive playing record at home came to an end, with Girling's becoming the first team to win at Central Park since 1947 as they mounted a successful run-chase in pursuit of a total of 160 after Graham Lockstone had posted 56 and Glyn Harvey had made 40. For once, the Blaina attack found wicket-taking difficult on their home patch and, although wickets tumbled when Girlings were in sight of victory, they reached their target with two wickets in hand.

1951 had seen Rumsey James take over as captain from Gomer Evans, and during the season the teacher at Glan-yr-afon Secondary Modern School produced some decent performances with bat and ball. However, the summer of 1951 also saw misfortune befall Rumsey and his family, ironically on his wife's birthday, as he was called away from a game at Central Park after hearing that his house was on fire. Mrs James, plus their two children, had also been watching the game but by the time they returned home, the house was completely gutted, with only a mattress and some clothes being salvaged from the charred remains. Rumsey had also been out for a duck during the match.

Despite these personal misfortunes, Rumsey was re-appointed as captain for 1952 as Blaina completed a fixture list which included matches against, amongst others, Lydney, Newport, Cardiff, Barry, RAF Hereford, Usk, Pontllanfraith plus the Bulwark club from Chepstow. James was still able to call on Gomer Evans' services, with the veteran posting an unbeaten 106 in the victory over Cardiff Polytechnic, besides taking 3/27 in the 25-run victory over Cross Keys. Most of his colleagues still came from the colleries as this

INTERNATIONAL CRICKET COMES TO BLAINA

The Eisteddfod notice in 1951

was a time when a group of miners were actively involved with the club, and at lunchtime on Saturday many workingmen hastily rushed home after their shift, quickly washed and then grabbed their whites in readiness for the afternoon game. None wanted to commit the *faux pas* enjoyed by some in other clubs of having dark black or grubby grey streaks on their whites, and the pre-match wash was a tangible sign that the working week was over, after which it was time for some enjoyment out under the summer sun before having a cold beer, or two, after play.

The Ash Tip Tests

During the 1950s the phrase Ashes Test Matches was given an entirely new meaning as the ash tips of Upper and Lower Cwmcelyn became the venue for matches played between the cricket-mad youngsters in the Blaina area. No indoor cricket school or practice nets for them, only the uneven bounce of the ash tip wicket and outfield!

> As Peter Jones remembers "the lads from White City – so called because of the white lime-painted fronts of the cottages – versus the boys from Waungron and Brynheulog. It was better than fighting, but these Test Matches were just as fiercely contested. There were umpires, scorers and refreshments. The upper Cwmcelyn ash tip was the home for the White City team, the lower Cwmcelyn ash tip the home for Waungron/Brynheulog team. Just a few bats, and no pads to protect against the speedily delivered corky ball off an uneven surface."
>
> These Tests produced many youngsters who went on to regularly play for Blaina – in addition to Peter Jones, the likes of Gareth Saunders, Roy Webber, Mike Amos, Ernie Kirkaldy, Dennis Williams and Brian Jenkins, all went on to play with great distinction for the club. The graduation to serious cricket held no fear for these players as they had played in many gripping Ashes Tests!

Blaina CC 1st XI 1951: Back row – Selwyn Parry, Herbert Williams, Rumsey James, D. Jones, Mostyn Williams, Glyn Harvey, Fred Hayter, Don Jones, Wyndham Preece, Ivor Williams. Middle Row – Albert Clarke, Bill (Colt) Davies, Ron Smith, Gomer Evans, Ron James, Ian Morgan. Front Row – Ernie Fearn and Graham Lockstone

INTERNATIONAL CRICKET COMES TO BLAINA

1953 saw international cricket come to Central Park as Blaina hosted a visit from the Pakistan Eaglets – a side containing a host of up-and-coming players from the sub-Continent who had been awarded Test status that summer. The fact that the Eaglets, who undertook a lengthy tour of the U.K., played at Blaina was another indication of the high-standing within cricketing circles that the club was held and, after a match against a West Indian XI at Ebbw Vale, the young Pakistani's headed to Central in the second week of August for a game against a combined Blaina and Brynmawr XI.

The Pakistani's batted first and Graham Lockstone dismissed Aleem-ud-din with the total on 31, before Fazal Mahmood and Billy Ibadullah took the total to 201 at lunch with a rapid second wicket partnership. Mahmood departed after the interval for 149, before Ikram Elahi took centrestage with a magnificent 130* as he added a further 252 runs before the Eaglets declared on 472/4. It continued to be something of a mismatch, as the tourists dismissed the combined XI for 130, with Don Jones top-scoring for the Blaina contingent with 28, as Saeed Ali and off-spinner Ebrahim Ghazali each claimed four wickets.

The game against the Eaglets was the highlight of the 1953 season – a summer which also saw Blaina defeat Abertillery in an exciting local derby with Mostyn Williams taking 5/33. It was also a red letter year for Capt. Evan Silk, the Head of Hafod-y-Ddol Grammar School, who had done so much behind the scenes to promote cricket, and other forms of healthy exercise, in the pupils under his charge. After 23 years as Headmaster, he was proudly able to announce in his end-of-year address at Prizegiving Day at Hermon Baptist Church that the school would shortly acquire a playing field.

A further boost for the cricket club came the following April when a fundraising rugby match was organised by Gomer Evans at Central Park. The contest – in aid of the Blaina club – saw an RAF side play a scratch XV chosen by Albert Jackson and comprising leading players from Abertillery, Ebbw Vale, Bristol and the Blaina rugby club. The game proved to be a decent contest and, with a dinner dance afterwards, it further swelled the club's coffers.

But other cricket clubs in the Monmouthshire Valleys were in a stronger financial position, especially neighbours Ebbw Vale, who had the backing of the local Welfare Association. Since 1946, Ebbw Vale had been staging annual County Championship matches and had forged close links with the county club who in the immediate post-war years, were running a Nursery and Development Programme across south Wales in an attempt to identify promising talent. Eugene Cross Park was one of the locations where a coaching programme was staged by the county's coaches, with Mel Gore and Dennis Williams being just two of the young Blaina lads to be invited to Ebbw Vale during the 1950s. Back in 1952, Gore had taken 4/9 on his debut for the 1st XI against Pontymister, and during the winter months he was amongst a group of forty promising young cricketers in Monmouthshire who received tuition and coaching from a number of Glamorgan players, plus Alan Fairfax of Australia and Maurice Tate, the former Surrey and England bowler.

Ebbw Vale were also able to secure the services of Harold Gimblett, the former Somerset and England batsman, on a five-year deal, and the presence of the Test batsman illustrated both the club's aspirations and standing in the Monmouthshire Valleys. They were also at the forefront of discussions about resurrecting an Eastern section of the South Wales and Monmouthshire League. Nothing came about, but the Blaina officials would have dearly loved to have been involved in the discussions.

Given the superior facilities and bank balance at Ebbw Vale, plus growing ambitions of League cricket, it would have been quite tempting for Gore and the other Blaina youngsters who ventured over to the neighbouring valley to switch allegiance. But Gore was a Blaina boy through and through and he remained loyal to the Central Park club forming, during the mid 1950s, a fine bowling alliance with Graham Lockstone. In 1954 the pair starred in a fine 79-run victory against Barry, whose side boasted two former Glamorgan players in Ernie Carless and Hubert Went, as well as several others with 2nd XI

Beynons CC in 1952

experience for the county side. The batting honours went to Blaina opener batsman Roy Dash who made a fine 71, before Gore and Lockstone tied down the Barry batsmen, with the latter taking 5/24 as Blaina dismissed the Barry side for just 75. The following year, the pair proved a real handful for the Abertillery side who were dismissed for 33. Lockstone claimed 5/21 and was well supported by Mel Gore who took 3/4 in the thrashing of local rivals.

Whilst some moved on, with Lockstone joining Panteg in the late 1950s, other promising players such as young batsman Mike Amos, remained loyal to Blaina and continued to ply their trade at Central Park. In Amos' case, he also continued to enjoy some light-hearted teasing that, as an opening batsman, he always walked out at the start of the game and took up the non-striker's position, simply because it allowed him the chance to quietly assess the strengths of the visiting new ball attack. In 1955 Amos had made a cultured innings of 78* in the draw against Barry, besides playing a match-winning innings against Abergavenny at Central Park, as his side turned the tables on the visitors who, earlier in the summer, had won at Avenue Road by dismissing Blaina for 49. The return contest proved to be a totally different affair as Lockstone claimed five wickets, before Amos anchored the run chase with an unbeaten 44 as Blaina won by five wickets. Amos' run-scoring during the 1950s drew the attention of Glamorgan's scouts and those selecting the Monmouthshire side. He did his cause no harm in 1958 when he was in the combined Abertillery and Blaina XI, along with Mel Gore and veteran Gomer Evans, who played the Glamorgan Colts at Abertillery.

Blaina could still call on the services of Rumsey and Ron James, who in 1954 recorded some standout performances in the match with Girlings as Blaina recorded a comprehensive 169-run victory. Rumsey posted a fine century, containing 9 fours and 7 sixes besides sharing a Club record stand of 162 with Ron James. Through their efforts, Blaina were able to declare on a formidable 267/7 before dismissing Girlings for 98. Also still available, and ever eager, was Kenny Cayford – another great character of Blaina cricket and a man who was involved in several humorous incidents both on and off the field.

Perhaps the funniest came in the match at the Llwynarthen ground near St. Mellons when Blaina met Cardiff YMCA. Kenny was chasing after the ball near the boundary before ending up tumbling over the ropes and into a thick patch of stinging nettles. His howls of pain soon indicated that he would be unable to continue fielding for a while and would require some attention to his midrift. The commotion drew the attention of a group of ladies in the pavilion who duly walked over and helped escort Kenny into the changing rooms, where they helped him onto a bed before applying bicarbonate of soda onto his thighs and lower stomach, as well as the area in between – though Kenny was not going to tell them about the lack of discomfort in his nether regions and, trying to supress the biggest of smiles, he allowed the ladies to treat his groin. It was no surprise that he had a few stories to tell on the team's journey back home, as well as trying to explain why he had been helped into the pavilion almost doubled up in pain before belatedly emerging with a broad smile after the closest of attention from his female admirers.

The winter of 1955/56 sadly saw the passing of two stalwarts of the Blaina Club, starting in late November with the death after a short illness of Arthur Lockstone, who had been the Blaina Treasurer for over a quarter of a century. Whilst never having the greater financial resources of neighbours Ebbw Vale or Abertillery, Arthur had meticulously ensured that the Blaina club never overstretched themselves, especially after the difficult years of the 1930s when the club nearly folded. The fact that they were still in existence, and enjoying success against some of the leading teams in south-east Wales was a measure of his careful management of the Club's finances.

Blaina's continued success in the 1950s was also a reflection of the efforts of Evan Watkins in the immediate post-war years in setting up the club again and galvanising local support after the absence of cricket for six years. Although he now lived in a prosperous Cardiff suburb, Watkins still remained close to the affairs of the Monmouthshire club and the performances of the new generation of Blaina stars brought a smile to his face when he visited Central Park to see the team in action. Sadly, his visits in 1955 were the last he made to his beloved club as, in January 1956 he died suddenly at his home in Bishops Road and, quite rightly, there was a massive contingent from Blaina at his funeral in Cardiff, paying tribute to the man who, above all else, had done so much to promote and nurture cricket at Central Park.

12
CRICKET ON SUNDAYS

The second half of the twentieth century therefore saw Blaina CC undertake their activities without their *eminence grise* EW Watkins. The decades from the 1950s onwards were very different to the years when Watkins had been playing with distinction for the club, and a number of sweeping changes took place to both local society and recreation in South Wales. Amongst the changes which started to affect the cricket club from the late 1950s were the increase in the number of longer, paid holidays which people were entitled to during the summer months, greater disposable

Blaina CC 1st XI 1956: Back row – Alan Clarke, Roy Webber, Colin Gilbert, Bryn Wiltshire, Howard Knight, Mike Amos. Front Row – Don Maidment, Gareth Saunders, Mel Morris, Gomer Evans, Don Jones. Umpire – Harry Niner

THE HISTORY OF BLAINA CRICKET CLUB

Blaina Wesleyan church

incomes, an increase in car ownership and personal mobility, as well as the emergence of organised sporting activities taking place on Sundays.

Quite what the grand old man of Blaina cricket would have made of the latter is not known as, like many of the Club's stalwart members, Watkins had been a regular at Berea Chapel. There had always been a strong link between the church and cricket in South Wales as, back in the late 18th century, cricket and other ball games had taken place in churchyards, as well as on common land or on the beaches close to the coastal settlements as the youngsters in the pre-industrial age amused themselves with various forms of recreation.

For many, many years, the thought of playing cricket on a Sunday had been an alien and abhorrent thought. For a start, Blaina was situated in one of the hotbeds of Nonconformism – a movement which in the 19th century had been strictly opposed to playing cricket on the Sabbath, with the devout Nonconformists believing that the playing of games, even at weekends was vain and inconsistent with the seriousness of life. The revelry and drunkenness that frequently accompanied the post-match celebrations were also frowned upon by those who supported the Temperance Movement, whilst other religious leaders felt that it was wrong for workingmen to fritter away their money gambling or drinking at matches, especially on Sundays.

> ### The Deadly Sin of Cricket!
>
> During the 19th century several religious leaders vehemently opposed the playing of cricket, especially on Sundays. In 1851 the Reverend P.M. Procter distributed a pamphlet amongst people living in the Monmouth and Forest of Dean areas in which he described how a miner called Thomas Morgan, who was normally first on the cricket ground, yet the last to return home, decided one Sunday to refrain from his heathen tendencies and drinking habits by going to church instead. According to the pamphlet, "he was immediately converted and never went near a cricket ground again. He died deeply penitent and Heaven gained a very good batsman."
>
> Similarly, in the 1870s the vicar of the Tabor Welsh Independent Church in Maesycymmer preached a sermon called "The Deadly Sin of Cricket", telling the congregation that "workingmen ought not to join themselves with gentlemen who had more money to spend, that it was a positive sin to go into a cricket field, that young men had no time to read their Bibles, all of their time being taken up in cricketing."

These religious barriers gradually declined during the second half of the nineteenth century following the growing popularity of the ethic of Muscular Christianity, and the writings of Charles Kingsley who advocated recreation as a means of bodily purification and practical Christianity. Moreover, there was a belief that brute strength and athletic power were good and godly characteristics, whilst physical weakness or a lack of exercise was synonymous with moral and spiritual inadequacy. Such views were handsomely illustrated in novels such as Tom Brown's Schooldays, with cricket and rugby football epitomising the benefits of manly exercise.

The upshot was that, across the booming settlements of South Wales during the late Victorian and early Edwardian era, many ministers saw no harm in encouraging their parishioners and choirboys to play, especially if it helped to increase attendances on Sundays and promoted moral and social reform. By the outbreak of the First World War, the Blaina district had become no different to other parts of England and Wales in having teams representing the local churches, chapels and Sunday schools including Nantyglo Wesleyans (formed in 1894), Blaina Congregational (1899), Nantyglo Holy Trinity (1900), Blaina Prims Methodist (1903), Blaina Salemites (1909) and Blaina Berea (1910).

Some of these church-based teams had been directly formed for an annual challenge with neighbouring parishes, or similar groups in neighbouring

THE HISTORY OF BLAINA CRICKET CLUB

Salem Baptist

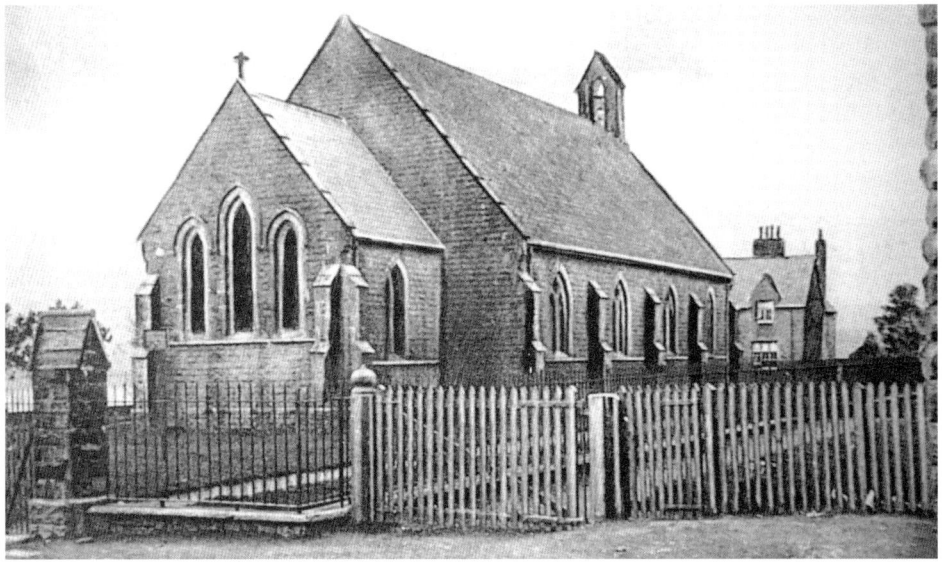

Holy Trinity Church

CRICKET ON SUNDAYS

Blaina Wesleyans CC in 1930

towns, whilst others arranged fixtures with local clubs, especially some of the junior teams in the locality. An example of the latter was the Blaina Salemites side who joined up with other local teams including Nantyglo, Winchestown and Garn in participating in the Western Valley Cricket League – created in 1908 – and played a regular round of matches alongside the likes of Abertillery, Aberbeeg, Ebbw Vale Coronets, Brynmawr and Ebbw Vale Primroses.

However, for all of these ecclesiastical sides and junior clubs in the early twentieth century, Sunday was still a day on which cricket, or any other form of recreation would not take place. Attitudes changed though after the Second World War and in the late 1950s, matches started to be played with growing regularity at Blaina on Sunday afternoons. At first, the games faced a few ribald comments, especially from the devout Chapel-goers and others who supported the views of the Lord's Day Observance Society who believed that no games should be played on the Sabbath. A few players, especially those with strong links with the local chapels were privately quite pleased on occasions when they failed to make the starting line-up in Sunday matches.

But the 1950s were a decade of great social change as new values and outlooks took hold in post-war Wales, and steadily the matches on Sunday afternoons grew in popularity with the club forming a Sunday XI where an emerging group of new players got further experience of 1st team cricket. These included bowlers Gareth Saunders, David Pope and Don Maidment, plus batsmen Roy Webber, Ernie Fearn, Mel Morris and wicket-keeper Dennis Williams.

A few old stagers were still around in the late 1950s, including Gomer Evans, who drew on all of his experience to help Blaina win a thrilling contest at Abergavenny in 1957 with victory secured with just two minutes to spare. Evans led the side in 1959 and 1960 before handing over the reins to Mel Gore and handing his kit to his wife, before allowing her to dispose of all of his whites with his wife believing (or perhaps secretly hoping!) that his playing days were finally over. Gomer though agreed to help out in an emergency, and one Saturday morning after a late withdrawal had occurred, he happily answered an SOS to play for the 1st XI. Mrs Evans quickly popped into the town's outfitters to purchase a brand new pair of whites for her beloved husband, but it did not prove to be the best of afternoons either for Gomer or his new trousers as whilst fielding he got his gleaming whites caught on the boundary fence, and after extracting himself he found huge rips and tears in his new kit. A couple of helping hands and borrowed kit got him through the game, but after stumps were drawn, he solemnly made his way home knowing what his wife was going to say after her efforts at getting him onto the field in the first place!

Mel Gore walking out to bat for Blaina

13
OVERCOMING THE DIFFICULTIES OF THE 1960S

By the 1960s, the boom years of the inter-war period were a distant memory. Back in the 1920s there had been forty teams in existence in the area between Llanhilleth and Nantyglo, with virtually every church and institution in the region, as well as several streets, boasting decent cricket teams. So popular was the game back in those years that matches were even staged on the hill tops and other areas of high, flat ground away from the crowded valley floors, with the contests between the region's premier teams attracting crowds of several thousand.

Blaina CC 1st XI 1960: Back row – Albert Clarke, Jim Garroway, Peter Jones, Don Maidment, Granville Griffiths, Roy Webber, Dennis Williams, Gareth Saunders, Mr. Harvey.
Middle row – Ernie Fearn, Bryn Wiltshire, Gomer Evans, Selwyn Parry, Don Jones, Mel Gore, Ivor Williams. Front row – Howard Knight and Mike Amos

It was a completely different story by the early 1960s when only several hundred enthusiasts turned up to watch contests such as Blaina against Abertillery. There were also just ten clubs in existence between Llanhilleth and Nantyglo, whilst teams often turned up for fixtures with just ten men. The sharp decline in interest and participation was a growing concern for all clubs in the Monmouthshire Valleys and in the South Wales Gazette of August 26th, 1960 the situation was summed up by the following:

> "It is not difficult to foresee a future in which little clubs will have quietly slipped out of existence, their use in creating spectator interest having been lost to a world of ultra-modern and manufactured entertainment."

Blaina were one of the clubs to face difficult times, and for them an added threat was the success of the neighbouring Dunlop Semtex club who had lured several promising players into their ranks. Mel Gore – who had led Blaina in 1961 and 1962 – switched allegiance in 1965 as he was appointed captain of the Semtex club. A carpenter at Beynon's colliery, Mel had played for Blaina since the age of fifteen, besides becoming captain of the Beynon's side that won the inter-colliery competition for three successive summers. A couple of the Blaina 1st XI and several of the club's 2nd XI also played for Beynon's whose games were therefore taken very seriously, especially when it came to the contest with Rose Heyworth who themselves had several Blaina players.

Mel Gore

OVERCOMING THE DIFFICULTIES OF THE 1960S

Mel was sorry to leave the Colliery, especially as there was great camaraderie amongst the miners and others employed at the pithead. But the wages were excellent with Dunlop and he celebrated his appointment as captain of the Semtex club by claiming a hat-trick against St. Fagans, taking 5/3 as the Cardiff-based club were dismissed for 47. It took Semtex batsmen Granville Ennis and Brian Aubrey just twenty minutes or so to swiftly see their side to victory.

This was one of several quite attractive fixtures for the Semtex side, who also met Abergavenny, Ton Pentre, Penarth, Barry Centurions and Cardiff 2nd XI, besides participating in the Dunlop inter-factory knock-out competition. The club had been formed as a result of another very important trend during the post-war era, namely the emergence of light industries in the Monmouthshire Valleys in a bid to arrest the problems of unemployment and prevent a reoccurrence of the problems experienced in the 1930s as the last vestiges of heavy industries and colliery-based activities underwent terminal decline. Indeed, the industrial landscape of the area underwent further change from the 1960s onwards as the remaining coal seams became exhausted and the last few supplies of iron ore became difficult to safely extract. Light industry increasingly replaced the mines and ironworks, with estates of factories springing up throughout the valley communities.

In 1965 the Semtex club also reached the finals of the Dunlop Inter-Factory Knock-out competition – a feat they also achieved again in 1966 with their successful summer being decorated by several standout performances from teenager Norman Bird. The young all-rounder enjoyed a fine game with both bat and ball against the Stewarts and Lloyds club from Newport, making an unbeaten 102 as he opened the batting, before taking a five-wicket haul as his side cruised to a comfortable win.

In contrast, Blaina were meeting with far less success, and their game in August 1964 away to Crickhowell summed up the state of the club during the 1960s. The home side batted first with their two openers coming close to sharing a double-century opening stand against Blaina's wholehearted, but largely ineffective attack. Not even the leonine veteran Don Maidment, who in 1960 had bowled unchanged to return figures of 7/51 against Abertillery, could claim a wicket as Crickhowell declared on 216/2. In contrast, Blaina wickets were soon tumbling when the visiting batsmen took to the crease and to make matters worse, Lyn Davies was unable to bat after being injured in the field. Blaina were soon dismissed for 67 as Crickhowell ran out winners of what had become a very one-sided contest by 149 runs.

Midway through the 1964 season, Blaina lost David Pope, their captain and leading fast bowler, who left the area to take up a teaching post in Southern England. He had served the Club well for over ten years, with

THE HISTORY OF BLAINA CRICKET CLUB

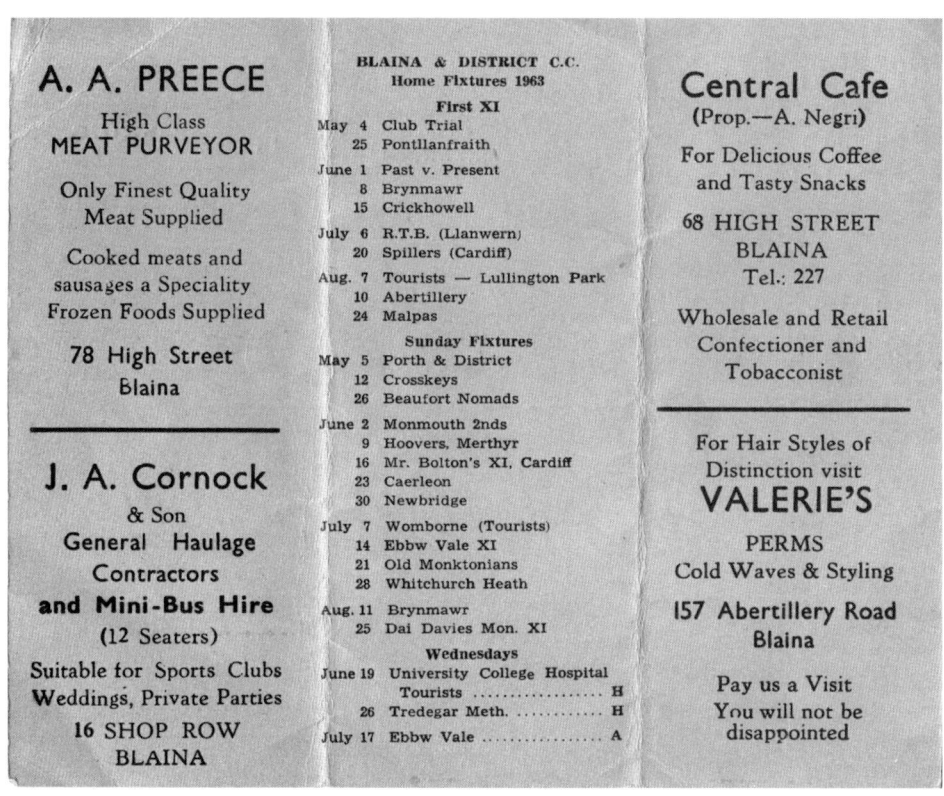

A fixture card for Blaina CC from the 1963 season

David Jones – the club's present Patron – valiantly stepping into his shoes. Further players and committee members, including Ivor Williams – the groundsman – all left to join the Semtex club. Following this exodus Ron Adams became Chairman and kept the club going aided by Ernie Fearn, Mel Morris and George Langley, with Malcolm Werrett as Head Groundsman.

In the absence of so many players from previous years, a number of new faces came to the fore, including batsmen Donald Saunders and John Walding, bowlers Keith Thomas, Norman Edwards and John Pratten, plus wicket-keeper Keith Dash. But they couldn't replace their experience, and the lack of playing success meant that the Blaina club sustained an overall loss at the end of three successive summers in 1966, 1967 and 1968. This had a snowball effect with the Blaina cricketers owing money to the Nantyglo and Blaina District Council for the rent of Central Park.

For a while, it seemed as if the town's cricket club was set to mirror the crumbling condition of St. Peter's Church, with masonry from the building – erected in the mid 19th century – tumbling through the roof in 1966 before

OVERCOMING THE DIFFICULTIES OF THE 1960S

Blaina 2nd XI 1964: Back Row – Howard Griffiths, John Walding, Ernie Fearn, Alan Williams. Umpire – Bryn Wiltshire. Middle row – David Jones, Gerry Prince, Keith Thomas, Maldwyn Brookes, Jack Brookes. Front row – Donald Saunders and Keith Dash

Blaina CC 1st XI 1965: Back row – Glyn Robinson, Dennis Williams, Ernie Fearn, Gomer Evans, Norman Edwards, Rumsey James, Don Maidment. Front row – David John, Keith Dash, Donald Saunders and Howard Knight

inspectors declared the structure unsafe and called for the church's demolition. But, unlike St.Peter's, the Blaina cricket club survived and went on to flourish, with their collective durability, plus the driving passion and determination of their leading players and officials, allowed the club to overcome the problems posed by these difficult years.

A lifeline was also thrown by the Nantyglo and Blaina District Council, who in 1969, wiped off the club's debts and did not call for the outstanding rent for Central Park. Instead, the council chairman Fred Griffiths said "the club's members are making a determined effort to pay their way." This news delighted Chairman Ernie Fearn and captain John Walding, with the club celebrating the Council's act of generosity by producing a decent performance in the opening home game of the season at Central Park. A defiant innings from Fearn meant that Pontnewynydd were set a stiff target of 161 in a shade over two hours. Graham Lockstone and youngster Alun Lewis were then in fine form with the ball, restricting the visitors to 116/7.

However, the modest funds meant that the wickets at Central Park were not always in the finest of conditions, with Blaina being dismissed for a mere 17 in May 1970 after winning the toss and electing to bat first in their local derby against Abertillery. This was certainly the nadir for Blaina and they were given a boost a few months later when both Mel Gore and Norman Bird returned from Semtex. Together with David John and Howard Knight, the pair provided added invaluable experience in the early 1970s as the Blaina club rebuilt their side in the Monmouthshire League after the difficulties of the 1960s. Gore's left-arm spin was virtually unplayable at Brynmawr in 1970 as he took 7/15, followed by 5/23 at Machen as Blaina secured another victory.

Two years later, Gore produced an outstanding all-round performance, top-scoring with 76 and taking 5/49 in the victory against Abercarn. Old stager Don ('Chocka') Maidment also continued to give his all, taking 8/45 against Radyr and Overseas in 1972, yet his efforts were not sufficient to pull off a victory for Blaina. John also demolished Machen in their encounter in 1970 at Central Park, taking 9/26 as Blaina eased to a comfortable victory, whilst Norman Bird made 57 and took 3/34 in the victory over Llantarnam in 1972. Howard Griffiths, a fine batsman and swing bowler, also played some excellent innings when captain in 1971, posting 93 against Abercarn and 76 in the contest with Cwmbran.

But the early 1970s was not all about the senior men as a number of young players progressed into the 1st XI. For example, Alun Lewis, after successfully captaining the 2nd XI, proved an effective opening bowler, taking 6/11 against Brynmawr at Central Park in 1970, whilst the following year Mike Pearce also produced some waspish spells including 5/38 in the away win at Abercarn. He followed this up in 1972 with 5/8 in the victory against Spencer Works and at

OVERCOMING THE DIFFICULTIES OF THE 1960S

Dunlop Semtex 1st XI 1970 – Back row – Dennis Tibbs, Granville Ennis, Brian Summers, Peter Addis, Derrick Haynes, Keith Williams. Middle row – Dennis Batten, Graham Cobourne, Howard Knight, Brian Aubrey. Front row – Tom Williams, Terry Cobourne, Eddie Hedges and Wilf Hunt

the end of the summer 6/46 against the touring Malvern Ramblers. Amongst the other youngsters to catch the eye in the early 1970s were Tony Edwards and Ioan Holmes, with the former proving to be a very useful all-rounder as he showed at Crumlin with a forceful innings of 63, followed by a waspish return of 4/17 against Llanyrafon. David Cobourne, a promising middle-order batsman, won selection in 1973 for the Monmouthshire Colts against their Glamorgan counterparts at Cwmbran, as well as the Monmouthshire Young Cricketers side in the Hilda Overy Trophy.

It proved to be a successful campaign for the young Monmouthshire cricketers as they defeated Glamorgan, Pembrokeshire, Gloucestershire and Leicestershire to lift the Trophy. It was a remarkable achievement for David and the Blaina club in general as the youngster, unlike some of the others in the Hilda Overy competition who had played a lot of county cricket at youth

Dai Cobourne

level and were already being tipped as future professionals, had never played any cricket at school and had been coached and nurtured entirely by the Blaina coaches.

Dai Cobourne Curry's Favour!

1973 saw David Cobourne taste – if that is the most appropriate word – some of the delights of *après cricket*. With plenty of encouragement from Don Maidment and other senior members in the Blaina side, the youngster agreed to join his older colleagues at an Indian restaurant in Cwmbran.

As he recalled in an interview for the *Taking the Field* Project, "I'd never been for an Indian meal before, but Don said I should try a vindaloo. Not knowing any different, and believing Don to be something of a connaisseur of curry, I accepted his advice. I duly managed to get through the meal, but when I got home I was in such a state that my mother banned me from cricket for a month!"

OVERCOMING THE DIFFICULTIES OF THE 1960S

But the Blaina club was struck a couple of grievous blows in the early 1970s as two of their most outstanding prospects were killed in motorcycle accidents in September and October 1972. Maldwyn Brookes was the first to be involved in a fatal accident as the 25 year-old mechanical engineer was killed on September 6th, 1972 as an untethered horse bolted into the road causing a motor cyclist to swerve up onto the pavement where he collided with the young cricketer.

Maldwyn's death meant that there were not many happy faces at the end-of-season jollities, and a month later Ken Rossiter also lost his life. Ken was a gifted young sportsman, shining also as a footballer, having progressed from the Blaina side to the Ebbw Vale club. Tragically, Ken's cricketing career with Blaina proved to be an all-to-brief one as in mid-October the 28 year-old was involved in an accident which cost the father of two his life. Ken was the pillion passenger on a motor cycle which was involved in a collision with a car in High Street, Blaina. The talented sportsman was taken to hospital in Abergavenny with a fractured skull and severe lacerations, but after a few hours at Nevill Hall he was transferred to the intensive care unit at Cardiff's Royal Infirmary. He never recovered and died two days after the accident.

14
REBUILDING IN THE 1970S

The loss of Maldwyn Brookes and Ken Rossiter within seven weeks of each other were cruel blows for the Blaina club and the local sporting community. But their fellow young cricketers responded in the course of the next few years with a number of eye-catching performances as the club successfully regrouped after the fallow years of the 1960s. Alun Lewis bowled Blaina to victory over Caerleon College in 1973 with a fine return of 4/22, followed the next year with 6/25 in the away win against Cardiff YMCA, as well as 5/26 in the victory over Abercarn. Mike Pearce also produced some outstanding spells including 6/25 and 4/5 in the wins in 1973 over Croesyceiliog and the Beaufort club from Ebbw Vale, whilst in 1975 his figures of 5/20 saw Blaina defeat Spencer Works.

Norman Bird was another to produce match-winning performances – with the ball, he took 4/33 and 5/38 to see Blaina to victory in 1973 over both Sofrydd and Tredegar Southend, whilst in 1975 he struck a combative 101 against Tredomen. Howard Griffiths added a hundred of his own the following weekend in the closing match of the 1975 season. The previous summer his useful away-swing bowling had yielded a return of 5/20 against Cardiff YMCA at Central Park as Blaina completed the double over the city-based team. In 1976, Griffiths came very close to hitting another century as he posted a fine 98 in the home win over Llanhilleth. Lyn Webber also took 6/29 in this victory, as well as 6/19 against Croesyceiliog, during what proved to be a quite modest summer for the Blaina club.

The Greatest Catch in Blaina's History

In 1976 a stunning catch was made at Llanyrafon by Bob Norster, and those who saw the athletic efforts of the Welsh rugby international still regard it as the best outfield catch they have ever seen by a Blaina cricketer.

Norster, who later won 34 rugby caps for Wales, appeared regularly for the Blaina side during the long, hot summer of 1976. he had been one of the promising young sportsmen at Nantyglo Comprehensive whose

REBUILDING IN THE 1970S

> competitive instincts and ball-playing skills were nurtured by Alan Davies who was a PE teacher at the school.
>
> He showed great promise as a fast bowler, and was duly encouraged to join Blaina CC along with his school colleague Martin Powell who also had the potential to develop into a decent all-rounder. Powell subsequently became a record, and prolific, points-scorer for Blaina RFC, whilst Norster – who took 4/18 in the victory over Pentwyn in 1976 – went on to become a British and Irish Lion, besides a leading administrator in regional rugby with the Cardiff Blues.

Gary Nicklin's batting proved invaluable on several occasions when runs were at a premium, making 73 and 54 in the two contests with Machen in 1976. Alan Brookes, the popular medium-pacer, also made telling contributions, with spells of 5/32 against Croesyceiliog and 4/30 in the contest with

Alun Barber (left) receiving an award

Llanwern. He subsequently played an important role in the late 1970s and early 1980s when his enthusiastic approach greatly assisted the development of the young bowlers who were coming through the ranks, with Alan always finding the time to pass on a few words of advice about bowling a good line and length.

Another local schoolmaster, Alun Barber, took over the captaincy of Blaina CC in 1977. The geography master at Hafod-y-ddol School was a talented all-round sportsman in his own right, representing Blaina at rugby in the winter, cricket in the summer, and giving plenty of his own time after school to coach and encourage his charges. His patient and enthusiastic efforts bore fruit in the following years as a number of his pupils went on to play for Blaina CC.

The club made headway under his leadership in 1977 with Howard Griffiths again producing some match-winning performances. He made 60 in the victory at Central Park over Llanhilleth, before starring with both bat and ball in the victory at Brynmawr, scoring 64 and taking 6/44. Two new faces in the 1st XI also helped to set up several victories with Chris Despres making 67, and Allen Hughes taking 6/51 in the win at Central Park over Croesyceiliog.

The same combination were also well to the fore in 1978 as Blaina enjoyed a superb run of nine successive victories, with their first defeat not coming until July 8th. The outstanding sequence began with a comfortable victory over Haven-on-the-Hill from Ynysddu as opening batsman Alan Cooper posted 82 whilst Howard Griffiths took 6/10. Chris Despres then top-scored in the home victory over Pentwyn before making a fine 73 in the away win against Pilkingtons. Another half-century from Alan Cooper, plus 6/87 from Allen Hughes saw Blaina to another win at home over the Old Monktonians side from Cardiff.

The series of victories was maintained as Allen Hughes claimed another five-wicket haul against the Orb Works team from Newport, before 66 from Chris Despres, supported by 6/25 from Lyn Webber whose off-cutters saw Blaina to another home win over Crumlin. In mid-June Allen Hughes took 6/13 to see Blaina to victory over ICI Pontypool, before an unbeaten half-century from Howard Griffiths maintained the unbeaten run against Centurions, another Newport-based club.

Tony Bytheway then posted 63 in the victory over Llanhilleth with his vibrant fifty being decorated by some rasping square-cuts. As a result, Blaina entered July still undefeated, but the following weekend the sequence ended at Pentwyn as the side crashed to defeat. They bounced back the following Saturday as captain Alun Barber led from the front with 6/24 in the win at Haven-on-the-Hill. In the next three weeks both Barry and Pilkingtons inflicted defeats over Barber's side, but the captain's seam bowling saw his side to two further victories in August, as he took 6/24 against the

REBUILDING IN THE 1970S

Howard Griffith batting in 1978

Old Monktonians before claiming 3/15 as Blaina rounded off the season at Central Park with another victory over Pilkingtons.

Blaina duly topped the League table – something that had not happened in over a decade – with an overall record of 13 wins from their 16 games. The 2nd XI under Gareth Gillingham also enjoyed a fine summer, with their skipper leading from the front as he posted back-to-back centuries against Llanyrafon and Newport, and looked like recording an unprecedented third the following weekend against Brynmawr before being dismissed for 74. Gillingham's individual success, as well as that of the 1st XI, led to the club deciding at their AGM in the Autumn of 1978 at the Old Hafodian Club to run a youth team in the Under 19 Gwent League – another decision that was to reap massive rewards in the subsequent years as a series of decent youngsters flourished for the Blaina club.

Redvers Price, Alan Williams, Gareth Gillingham and David Gomery agreed to oversee, coach and manage the youth side and, to their credit, the

David Gomery

side made a tremendous start in 1979, beating their counterparts from Panteg, Abergavenny, Sudbrook, Croesyceiliog and Ebbw Vale, before travelling to Rodney Parade and registering a decisive six-run victory over Newport. In all, the youth side were unbeaten in nine games and accumulated the highest number of points in the League, but in order to be the champions, the rules stated that ten matches needed to be played and this honour went elsewhere, much to the chagrin of the Blaina club.

Chris Despres, a history teacher at Nantyglo Comprehensive, took over the captaincy of the 1st XI in 1979. He had been a fine acquisition for the club at the start of the 1977 season and the attractive stroke-maker brought to the leadership his experience of League cricket in the Manchester area. Although Blaina recorded six victories, 1979 did not prove to be quite as successful a summer as the previous year. Nevertheless, they recorded four wins in succession during June, with the winning sequence being kick-started by a fine half-century against Orb Works from Norman Bird, who had returned to Blaina after a spell at Abertillery. After the Old Monktonians had been beaten, Blaina maintained their winning ways against Raglan with Alun Barber taking 4/9 and Allen Hughes 4/18 including four wickets in successive balls. The

REBUILDING IN THE 1970S

Central Park in 1979

following weekend, Norman Bird helped to make it four in a row as he took 8/27 as the Centurions went down to a heavy defeat.

Alan Williams, the loyal Blaina wicket-keeper, still holds fond memories of the 1979 season as this was the summer when it looked like he would score a century for his beloved side at Central Park. However, he was dismissed when eight runs short of his coveted hundred, but his efforts still allowed Blaina to round off their season at home with a resounding win against the Old Monktonians. Williams was disappointed to have missed out but the following summer, the doughty gloveman posted a century for the Blaina side making 118 in the match away to Orb Works.

The 189-run victory against the Newport-based side was the highlight of the season for the Blaina club, with Alan Williams and Tony Bytheway adding 184 for the first wicket – the highest-ever league opening stand in the history of the club. Bytheway was eventually dismissed for 70 before teenager Alan Cooper came in to post a quickfire 54 as Blaina ended their 45 overs on 292/2. The home side were never in the hunt as Alun Lewis made inroads with the new ball, before ending with figures of 4/29, whilst Alun Barber chipped in with 4/38 as Blaina posted a comprehensive victory.

THE HISTORY OF BLAINA CRICKET CLUB

Action from the game between Blaina and Brynmawr in 1978

Blaina v Brynmawr in 1978

REBUILDING IN THE 1970S

Not out! Gary Nicklin remains at the crease after a dropped catch in 1978

The Boy Who Scored 600, Approximately!

The school holidays of the summer of 1978 were exactly as they should be – warm, dry and sunny, and perfect for cricket. A dozen boys from Coedcae duly took the opportunity to play their own version of Test Match cricket on the outfield of Central Park at the rugby ground end. Groundsman Alan Williams officiated as timekeeper with play starting each day at 11.25, with dinner at 1pm, tea at 3.45pm and close of play at 5 o'clock.

This particular summer saw games between England and the West Indies, with Clive Cooper leading the England six and Karl Teague the West Indies team, and one particular contest during the sun-baked summer saw an astonishing performance from the England captain as Clive Cooper batted for almost three and a quarter days!

Having posted his century on the opening day, Clive moved on to an unbeaten 350 – with fine support from Graham Seabrook – as his side reached a mammoth 425/2. Rather than declare, Clive continued his innings on day three and by close of play was roughly 580 not out as the scorer had run out of paper! Fresh supplies were brought the next day as Clive continued to 600, whereupon a large appeal for l.b.w was upheld and his monumental innings ended. He immediately declared, although there was some dispute as to precisely how many both he and his side had made. Karl Teague then opened the batting some twenty minutes before lunch wondering whether he could emulate his opposite number, but he had his middle stump uprooted first ball by a perfect Yorker from Gareth Langridge. "Can I have another go please?" was his sorrowful request as the England side celebrated, before telling him that he would have to wait until the follow-on. He did though have the final laugh as heavy rain fell after the interval washing out the rest of a quite remarkable game!

15
A RETURN TO THE PREMIER DIVISION

The success on the field in the late 1970s meant that the Blaina club was in a far more healthier position at the start of the 1980s than they had been ten years before. The buoyant mood with the club was reflected in the excellent attendance at winter nets in 1979/80 as well as the building work at Central Park, where a new pavilion with showers and a tea room, was in the process of being erected in readiness for the 1980 season.

As Chris Despres recalls, "in 1976 the players used to emerge from a pavilion that was a green shack. It's only facility was running water, and from it's ramshackle state, one would think that it had been erected in the 19th century in the times of Crawshay Bailey! The outfield was seldom cut and the pitch, full of weeds and ruts, was an appalling playing surface. Wallowing near the bottom of Division Four of the Gwent Leagues, the prospects were bleak – no promising youngsters, older players serving out time, and financial disaster always imminent. From that low ebb of despair, the club was rescued by the efforts of two men – Alan Williams and Alun Lewis."

Indeed, it was under Alun Lewis' captaincy in the early 1980s that Blaina enjoyed another purple patch. He was in charge between 1981 and 1983, as the club more than capitalised on the headway made in the previous few years, with the 1st XI winning eight games in Division One of the Gwent Cricket League games and ten friendlies in 1981, followed by eight League wins in 1982 to end up as runners-up in Division One and earning promotion back into the Premier Division in 1983.

Alun Lewis led from the front with the ball in 1981 – his first year in charge – taking 6/33 against Crickhowell and 4/30 in the victory over Cardiff YMCA. Alun Barber claimed 7/11 in the win over Llanyrafon, whilst promising teenager Darryl Davies contributed to a pair of victories, with 5/34 against Machen and 3/22 against Spencer Works. Darryl was another youngster to have been encouraged to play by Alun Barber and other teachers at Hafod-y-ddol School, before being nurtured in the youth section of the Blaina club.

Indeed, this period increasingly saw the guiding influence of several local schoolteachers, including David Gomery, Alun Barber and Gareth Eacott,

Alun Lewis (left) as Darryl Davies receives an award

which, together with the paternalistic attitude of several senior members of the Blaina club, helped to identify and groom the next generation of Blaina cricketers. Nurturing minors as opposed to nurturing miners became the mantra for the town club who in the past had found the local collieries and their cricket teams to be a fertile breeding ground for spotting emerging talent. By the 1970s the industrial landscape had taken a turn for the worse as a round of colliery closures took place with the productive coal seams becoming increasingly expensive, and difficult, to obtain. The local economy took another hit with the closure of the Semtex plant as a result of a major scare over the release of harmful asbestos dust. Several workers at the plant subsequently died and the closure of the Semtex works only added to the growing pool of unemployed men in the Monmouthshire valleys.

Whilst much of the local industry was poised to enter a trough of terminal decline, the fortunes of the Blaina cricket club were steadily on the up. During the next few years, both the 1st XI and the 2nd XI met with much success, with

A RETURN TO THE PREMIER DIVISION

the youngsters playing in the latter side benefitting from the likes of John Wright, whose vast experience and all-round skills, were of great assistance as the youngsters cut their teeth in senior cricket. Paul Brookes – the son of Alan Brookes – was one of the youngsters who plied his trade to great effect in the Seconds before emerging as a belligerent batsman with the 1st XI.

As far as the 1st XI was concerned, several batsmen enjoyed much success in 1981, most notably Alan Cooper. He enjoyed an outstanding summer, posting a pair of forthright centuries at Central Park with 108 against Machen and 101 against Old Monktonians. Chris Despres was also in decent form, making 93 in the victory at Llanyrafon, whilst Paul Williams produced two match-winning innings with 84 in the victory over Haven-on-the-Hill and 70 in the away win against Spencer Works.

This good form was continued in 1982 as Alun Lewis led Blaina to the runners-up spot in Division One to secure promotion back into the Premier Division of the Gwent Cricket League. Whilst it was largely a team effort, it would be wrong not to attribute much of the success to the excellent batting of Alan Cooper, who enjoyed a fine season and attracted the attention of the county selectors. He struck 80 and 66 in the wins against Cardiff YMCA, 77 and 88 against Machen and a superb 95 in the penultimate game of the season with Brynmawr which helped to clinch promotion. In fact, Brynmawr must have been sick of the sight of Alan Cooper as, earlier in June, he had taken 6/59 to see Blaina to victory.

On the bowling front, some of the best spells came from Darryl Davies, whose lively seam bowling included a return of 9/48 against Spencer Works in a match which remarkably Blaina failed to win. He was also on the losing side in the friendly against Haven-on-the-Hill in which he took 6/26, but there were plenty of occasions where his waspish bowling helped to put Blaina on the way to victory, including a return of 5/15 at Central Park against Tredomen. Promotion to the Premier League was clinched on August 21st with a 29-run victory at Llanyrafon.

To prepare for the fresh challenge of Premier Division cricket, Blaina's cricketers spent the winter of 1982/83 participating in the National Vendors Indoor League at Ebbw Vale Leisure Centre. Tredegar Cavaliers, Ebbw Vale, Dowlais, Brynmawr, Pontnewynydd, Abergavenny, BSC, Abertillery and Beaufort were the other participants in the 18-match six-a-side competition which saw Blaina end up in fifth place with the rising stars of the club performing with credit. David Gomery, Mark Davies, Darryl Davies, brothers Alan and Clive Cooper, plus schoolboy wicket-keeper John Prisk all produced some excellent performances in the Indoor League. Indeed, their efforts stood them in good stead as they duly formed the backbone of the Blaina side in the summer of 1983.

THE HISTORY OF BLAINA CRICKET CLUB

Darryl Davies bowling at Ebbw Vale in 1999

Darryl Davies showed the benefit of his winter efforts at Ebbw Vale by taking 6/16 in the early season friendly against Beechwood, but rain then played havoc with the opening month of League contests. When the Blaina side eventually got onto the field in early June, Darryl Davies shared a match-winning stand of 74 with Alan Cooper as the Premier new boys opened their account by beating Llanarth.

This was the first of many excellent innings once again by Alan Cooper who enjoyed another productive summer, amassing 639 runs and four League hundreds. His highest score of a fantastic season was 156 against Croesyceiliog, whilst he also posted back-to-back hundreds against Pontnewynydd and Monmouth. In the first contest, Cooper's efforts saw Blaina to 242/7 against an attack who boasted Brian Williams who was regarded as the fastest and most feared bowler in the League. Before the match he had – in Fred Trueman style – let all the visiting batsmen know how he was going to create havoc in the Blaina line-up. But Alan Cooper had other ideas and he soon scored a flurry of boundaries against the paceman who, by a great coincidence, then started to complain of a tight hamstring and retired from the attack!

A RETURN TO THE PREMIER DIVISION

Pontnewynydd subsequently mounted a spirited run chase before some typically accurate bowling from Darryl Davies and Steve Williams – who steadily developed into a useful new ball bowler as the season progressed – blunted their progress and with some shrewd captaincy from Alun Lewis, Blaina eased to a 23-run victory.

Blaina also enjoyed a couple of even narrower victories, each by two wickets, as Caerleon were beaten after some decent performances with bat and ball by the Cooper brothers. Whiteheads were also defeated by the same margin with Alan Cooper taking 4/12, before a level-headed innings by Darryl Davies anchored Blaina's run chase and saw them to victory. They also lost in the penultimate over against Newport Fugitives, but went down to a more resounding 104-run defeat against Newbridge as they ended the season in a respectable fifth place.

Blaina also enjoyed some success in the various knock-out competitions in 1983. In the Welsh Girobank Cup, they defeated BSC Ebbw Vale in the opening round, with Alan Cooper posting a match-winning half-century. His bowling was to the fore in the second round against Tredegar Cavaliers as he took 4/16 and was ably supported by Roy Mogford who claimed 3/11. George Morgan – the finest fielder in the side – held onto a couple of superb catches before Clive Cooper steered Blaina to a four-wicket victory.

Malpas ended Blaina's winning run in the 40-over competition, but Blaina reached the final of the Gwent League Cup – a 20-over competition, comprising a series of evening games in midweek. After defeating Girlings, Blaina overcame Spencer Works in the second round, with Darryl Davies taking 4/14 and Clive Cooper posting 49. Blaina duly defeated Sudbrook in a nail-biting semi-final, before losing to Abertillery. They were also runners-up in the Monmouth Sixes, losing to Ross-on-Wye in the final, as well as in the Blaenau-Gwent Sixes as the clubs in the region instigated a series of six-a-side competitions, largely on Sundays.

There was further good news later in the summer as the Blaina club received a decent grant from the Blaina Reading Institute Charitable Trust Fund. It's award stemmed from the support of Ernie Barber – a lifelong supporter of the town club and an employee for over forty years at the colliery – who had become secretary of the Trust and was only too happy to assist the sporting community as the local economy continued to decline.

Despite ending up as runners-up in these three competitions, it had been another successful summer for the Blaina team. However, Alun Lewis and Alan Williams, were each affected by illness during the summer and in Lewis' case, it forced him to stand down as captain for 1984. Alun Barber took over the reins as Blaina further consolidated on their recent headway, finishing one place higher in fourth spot in the League table, and all after an early

THE HISTORY OF BLAINA CRICKET CLUB

The Blaina CC side that took part in the six-a-side competition at Monmouth in 1983. Back row – Steve Williams, David Cobourne, Dick Williams. Front row – John Prisk, Darryl Davies and Alan Cooper

season injury crisis had seen David Cobourne and Glyn Bayton come out of retirement to play again for the 1st XI against Blackwood. It proved to be a happy return as Darryl Davies, despite ankle and knee ailments, took 5/19 in 11 overs as first change to restrict Blackwood to 147. Blaina then slipped to 60/5 before Clive Cooper blasted an unbeaten 65, smashing 11 fours and 2 sixes to see his side home.

With injuries still affecting the side, a series of defeats then followed, although Blaina might have won against Sudbrook had it not been for a dramatic collapse after some tailend hitting by the visitors. Mike Keogh struck four sixes in one of the closing overs for Sudbrook to leave Blaina chasing 176. At 117/1 with Alan Cooper posting another feisty fifty, they seemed in a decent position, but a dramatic collapse then ensued as they ended up ten runs short.

A century from Alan Cooper saw Blaina return to winning ways against Pontnewynydd, with the opening batsmen also taking 7/57 with his seamers against Llanarth to see Blaina to victory against the side that had been leading the table. The Cooper brothers and Darryl Davies all made useful contributions with bat and ball in the victory over Newport Fugitives, before Davies claimed 9/43 in a remarkable spell in the friendly at Barry over the August Bank Holiday. Chasing 107, Clive Cooper blasted a quickfire 75* including four sixes in an over as Blaina raced to a seven-wicket victory. The pair also produced standout performances in the end-of-season victory against Croesyceiliog, with Cooper posting 79* and Darryl Davies taking 6/46 as Blaina clinched fourth place in the table. It was another measure of Blaina's healthy progress as Croesyceiliog had sufficient financial resources to secure the services of Steve Watkins, the former Worcestershire batsman.

It was perhaps no coincidence that this golden era, between 1984 and 1988, also coincided with the presence of Brian Sillman as club chairman. He proved to be an impartial and constructive figurehead, with the fund-raising efforts of a bed-push to Nevil Hall Hospital being an example of his foresight and initiative. During this period, Blaina were also able to call upon wise words of advice from the likes of Redvers Price, who had been skipper of the 2nd XI and Sunday side in the 1970s. Like Brian, Redvers has been closely associated with the club over the past five decades, serving as Chairman in 1995 and 1996 and, in recent times, willingly undertaking the duties of 1st XI umpire.

Memorable Matches by Darryl Davies

Number 4 – Blaina v St.Fagans in the Welsh Girobank Cup, May 20th, 1984

This game has been included because of the bizarre sequence of events which culminated in a ten-over thrash in virtual darkness, with street lights on and car headlights illuminating the playing area on Central Park. Several hours earlier Blaina had been eagerly anticipating the arrival of their opponents from one of the best club sides in Welsh cricket for the Girobank Cup match. Blaina cricket was on an upward curve and the chance of a famous win over the St.Fagans men was a possibility.

Blaina were asked to bat first and got off to the worst possible start by losing David Gomery, Alan Cooper and Chris Despres to the left-arm spin combination of David Painter and Tony Smith. At 34–3 some rebuilding was required and Clive Cooper and John Prisk duly brought Blaina back into the game with a half-century stand, before Dick Williams also gave Prisk some excellent support.

At 115–6 a storm of near Biblical proportions descended on Central Park and set in motion a chain of events which nearly saw the first day-night cricket match in Wales. The torrent of rain flooded the playing area and after an early tea was taken, the 40-over match was abandoned.

Arrangements were made for a re-match, but these were complicated by the fact that St.Fagans were engaged in a Haig Village Cup contest the following weekend.

With the storm seemingly having passed, St.Fagans skipper Ricky Needham sportingly enquired if Blaina fancied a ten over slog on the artificial wicket which had been installed eighteen months earlier. After some deliberation in the home changing room, the offer was accepted and frantic telephone calls were made to the rugby club to see if their floodlights could be used, as cars were placed around the boundary edge to provide some supplementary illumination.

Rain started to fall as, for the second time in the day, the Cooper brothers made their way to the wicket to face Phil Makinson and Stuart Robertson. Alan Cooper duly anchored the innings as he steered Blaina to 73–3 in their ten-over allocation. The rain intensified as the visitors began their innings and, with the turf in a saturated state, hitting fours along the ground was virtually impossible. The Blaina bowlers though found that the ball was akin to a bar of soap, and when Needham flayed a massive six onto the rugby ground, it put St.Fagans in pole position.

But Allen Hughes then produced his infamous "dambuster" delivery which on the second – or maybe third – bounce bowled Needham for 32. With David Mason still working the ball around, the equation became five runs from the final over which was bowled by Alan Cooper. Two singles, two dot balls and a run out then followed off the first five balls, before Mason nudged the last ball down to short third man. Despite being just twenty yards away, the fielder could not quickly scoop up the sopping wet ball and Mason scrambled back for a fortuitous second run to leave the contest tied. But in the dry of the changing rooms and, with the rule books at the ready, St. Fagans were deemed the winners by virtue of losing fewer wickets.

Blaina team – Alan Cooper, Clive Cooper, Chris Despres, Dick Williams, Steve Williams, John Prisk, Allen Hughes, Alan Williams (wkt), David Gomery, Ralph Edmunds and Peter Knapper.

16
THE RESURRECTION OF TOURS

Blaina's success in the Gwent Leagues during the 1980s, and their improving financial situation, led to the resurrection of an annual tour. After many years in abeyance, 1983 saw an intrepid band of Blaina cricketers, led by tour captain Chris Despres, travel by minibus up the M5 to play Catford Wanderers. As the captain later recalled, "we left at 6 a.m. for the journey up to London after the squad had had an early night – it proved to be the last they would have for a few days, although Dai Cobourne was to show how life could be lived without sleep – the nearest he got to sleeping was having a night cap!"

The party included guest off-spinner Bob O'Brien from Brynmawr, and he played a crucial role in the tour opener against Catford, taking 5/32 in eleven overs as the home side failed in their pursuit of 179. Blaina's victory on English soil was then accompanied in time-honoured fashion of cricket tours with plenty of revelry, singing and drinking with their opponents until the early hours. To add to the colour and character in the Catford clubhouse, behind the bar was a former professional wrestler called Bob who regaled the visitors with tales of his bouts with Welshman Adrian Street. If these graphic stories from the world of grunt and groan were not enough, the Blaina cricketers then rounded off the night by visiting an East End nightclub, which apparently had close affiliations with the legendary Kray twins.

Not surprisingly, there were plenty of headaches and tired limbs the next day in Beckenham, with one of the most spritely figures being 63 year-old Ernie Fearn who had come out of retirement for the tour. The second contest saw the intrepid Welshman in action against a side drawn from staff at the local Post Offices. To make matters worse for those nursing headaches and hangovers, the local side won the toss and opted to bat first as the tourists endured a difficult first hour in the field. But O'Brien then came to their rescue as, together with Darryl Davies, they induced a late tumble of wickets. But the task of chasing 150 was too much after the excesses of the previous evening, as Blaina slumped to 27/6 before Dick Williams and John Prisk gave their total a modicum of respectability.

The village of Stone in Gloucestershire was the final destination as the merry tourists made their way back towards home. Once again, the bowling

Chris Despres

of O'Brien and Davies was to the fore as the Gloucestershire side were dismissed for 116. Mark ('Fudge') Davies then struck a vibrant fifty as Blaina won by five wickets. Their record of two wins out of three, together with the camaraderie and other after-hours jollifications, meant that there were plenty interested in going on the 1984 tour in the second weekend of September.

Once again, Chris Despres was tour captain as the Blaina side travelled by minibus up the M5 to play Catford Wanderers, before travelling to Lord's to watch the NatWest Trophy final, followed by a journey back west along the motorway and north up the M5 to Cheltenham where they met the Civil Service side drawn from staff employed at the GCHQ complex. In the opening game, Clive Cooper struck a rapid 81 as Blaina declared on 205/6. Darryl Davies then claimed five wickets as Catford lost wickets at regular intervals before shutting up shop on 180/9. The next day, Blaina batted first against the Cheltenham side, but it seemed that the travelling might have caught up with them as they slipped to 73/8 before Chris Despres engineered a stubborn fight-back to see Blaina to 140. Darryl Davies and Dick Williams then claimed early wickets before Clive Cooper claimed 4/6 as Blaina rounded off their short tour with a four-run win.

It proved to be such a popular venture that it was extended the following year with the tour at the end of August 1985 comprising another match against Catford Wanderers, as well as matches with South Surbiton and Stone in Gloucestershire. Once again, Chris Despres led the Blaina players on their visit to the Home Counties with the tour captain posting a half-century as Catford were defeated. However, south Surbiton ran out victors the following day, before Mark Davies made a century against Stone as Blaina's touring side posted their second victory on English soil. Davies remained in decent form as the following day the Blaina side met Monmouth, but his 80 could not seal a victory.

Further tours took place to Oldham and Bournemouth, with the former largely being a social trip without any cricketing activity. Once again, these

THE RESURRECTION OF TOURS

Blaina CC 1st XI 1986: Back Row – Alan Cooper, Darryl Davies, Lyn Prisk, Alan Williams, John Prisk, Des Norton. Front Row – Ralph Edmunds, Alun Barber, Steve Williams, David Morgan and Mark Davies

tours were memorable for the revelry and evening antics, which included an arm-wrestling encounter in Bournemouth between Roy Mogford, and an Irishman who, according to local legend had never lost a contest. But forty-five minutes with Blaina's very own strongman saw the local hero lose his unbeaten tag and, so impressed was he with Roy and the rest of the party, that he subsequently joined them as their minder for the rest of the tour. Chris Despres had been the driving force behind these tours, but from 1985 he worked in Cardiff and, with less time to plan these visits, the tours died out in the late 1980s.

1985 also saw 21 year-old Darryl Davies take over the captaincy. At the time, he was the youngest player to be given this honour, and the youngster saw the 1st XI and the Sunday XI record ten successive victories in May and June. The fantastic sequence began with Mark Davies making 82 for the Sunday side against Rhymney, before Steve Williams took 6/30 to see Blaina to a League victory over Pontnewynydd. Fifties by Mark Davies, Clive Cooper, Chris Despres and David Gomery saw Blaina to well-earned victories over Blaenavon, Tredegar Southend, Spencer Works and Beechwood.

THE HISTORY OF BLAINA CRICKET CLUB

Darryl Davies

Darryl Davies has played with distinction for Blaina 1st XI over four decades and, during his career, he claimed over a thousand wickets for the club. He reached this major landmark in the final League match of the 2007 season, as he took 5/15 against Bridgend, with his first victim – Steve Richmond – being caught by wicket-keeper Daniel Edwards to give the stalwart of the club his 1,000th wicket for the club.

A special presentation subsequently took place with the match ball being mounted on a plinth and awarded to Davies by Club President Martin Witherall. In handing over the special memento Martin thanked Darryl for all of his hard work over a quarter of a century bowling up the slope into the wind from the rugby ground, besides hoping that his second thousand would come a bit quicker than the first!

Darryl Davies (right) receives a special presentation to mark his haul of 1,000 wickets for the club

The sequence of wins however ended with defeat away to Barry, but a career-best 134 from Clive Cooper, aided by 5/35 from Steve Williams, saw Blaina return to winning ways in the local derby at Central Park against

Abertillery. Williams' stump-to-stump seam bowling had been a fine acquisition and his love of long spells, as well as his accuracy on damp surfaces, gave Blaina's attack an important cutting edge. But it was their batsmen who laid the foundation of several victories as a few weeks later, 122 by Mark Davies saw Blaina to victory in the friendly with Cardiff Mitre, whilst another team from the Welsh capital – the Old Monktonians – were beaten thanks to 96 from Clive Cooper.

Off the field, 1985 was an extremely difficult year with the prolonged Miners' Strike and the subsequent closure of various collieries. The good form of the cricket club during the summer months helped many Blaina men to take their minds away from the union unrest and the other traumas caused by unemployment. As at other times in the club's history, the increasingly fractured industrial relations brought the community together, and this enhanced feeling of comradeship benefitted the club. The winter of 1985/86 duly saw plenty of activity from the Blaina cricketers with the club winning the Blaenau Gwent Indoor Six-a-side competition staged at Ebbw Vale Leisure Centre. Alan Williams and the club's other coaches also oversaw a series of coaching sessions at Nantyglo Comprehensive School. Ten years before, local journalists had been predicting the demise of cricket in the area but, once again for 1986, Blaina were able to field five teams with a 1st XI, 2nd XI, Sunday XI, Midweek XI and a Youth XI.

However, the season saw Blaina, now under the captaincy of Steve Williams, slip to the lower part of the table with the club involved in a relegation battle with Caerleon. The summer began poorly as Blaina were dismissed for 22 by Sudbrook. This had been the first-ever match at Sudbrook's new ground, as well as being the debut of a Blaina youngster called Wayne Nash, then the apprentice groundsman at Central Park under Alan Williams, who went on to become groundsman at Ninian Park, the home of Cardiff FC, as well as stadium manager at the recently created Cardiff City Stadium.

A few weeks later Alan Cooper posted 97 against Monmouth, but Blaina lost again by seven wickets as the visitors chased the target on a another shirt-front wicket at Central Park prepared by Alan Williams. John Prisk, who had posted some decent scores in the course of the past few years, then made an unbeaten 105 in the victory over Pontnewynydd, before the following week Mark Davies made 76 as Blaina defeated Sudbrook.

Defeats then followed against Newbridge and Croesyceiliog, with the weather also intervening in some games, including the penultimate match of the season as fellow relegation strugglers Caerleon visited Central Park. But, just as Blaina appeared to be getting on top, rains washed out the contest and Blaina's fate went to the final weekend when a victory at Monmouth clinched their survival as Caerleon lost against Newport Fugitives. Blaina

THE HISTORY OF BLAINA CRICKET CLUB

had met with some success as well in the various cup competitions, beating Caerphilly in the Welsh Girobank Cup thanks to the Prisk brothers, with John making 58 and Lyndon 46. Pontymister were then dismissed in the second round, before Blaina slipped to defeat at Barry despite a fighting fifty from Mark Davies. The latter also struck a fine 107 in Blaina's victory over Shirenewton in the Gwent League cup, but his side went down to defeat in the next round.

Blaina however met with much success in the Indoor League in the winter of 1986/87 as, for the second successive winter, they won the competition at Ebbw Vale, and put together an unbeaten sequence comprising all 18 matches of the competition to lift the trophy again. Their success was based on a series of fine performances from Steve Williams, Darryl Davies, the Cooper brothers, Roy Mogford, Lyndon Prisk and Andrew Palmer.

Alan Williams returned to 1st XI action in 1987 and achieved a lifelong ambition by leading the side. It did not though prove to be a successful summer, as the club enjoyed mixed fortunes and ended up being relegated to division two. The year had not begun well as Chris Despres left the area following his promotion to a teaching post in a Cardiff school. He subsequently joined St. Fagans and enjoyed decent success with the village side from the outskirts of the Welsh capital.

The Blaina team that won the Blaenau Gwent Indoor League competition in 1987. Back row – Alan Cooper, Gareth Hughes, Allen Hancock, Darryl Davies. Front row – Andrew Palmer, Clive Cooper, Mayor Harry Evans, Roy Mogford and Lyn Gore

THE RESURRECTION OF TOURS

To make matters worse, Clive Cooper's work commitments also restricted his availability, whilst Mark Davies left to join Brynmawr. In the absence of three important players, it was no surprise that Blaina lost their first three League games to Llanarth, Sudbrook and Brynmawr, despite some fine innings from Alan Cooper who struck 67 and 97 against the latter pair of opponents. Alan Cooper's bowling, in tandem with Darryl Davies, saw Blaina open their account for the summer as Newbridge were beaten by 6 runs. A haul of 6/65 by Cooper could not see his side to victory against Machen, but a five-wicket haul by Davies set up a victory over Monmouth.

Newport Fugitives were then defeated as the Cooper brothers shone with bat and ball, and Blaina were grateful for another half-century from Alan Cooper against Machen, but they slipped back to the Second Division. Blaina also met with little success in the knock-out competition, losing to Brecon in the Welsh Girobank Cup despite 64 from Darryl Davies, whilst in the Gwent League Cup, they were beaten by Sudbrook even though Steve Williams took 6/8. They did, however, defeat Weston-super-Mare in a friendly at Central Park. It was the first time that the Somerset side had visited Blaina and they looked to be in the ascendancy after declaring on 232/4. However, Blaina won with two wickets and two balls to spare thanks to a superb 133 from Clive Cooper and an unbeaten 74 by John Prisk which guided Blaina home in the final over of what had proved to be an enthralling contest.

Around this time Allen Hancock joined the Blaina club. He duly became a permanent fixture in the line-up in the course of the next fifteen years or so, with his commitment and loyal service – plus his knack of picking up wickets at vital times – being greatly appreciated by his colleagues. He also worked very hard for the club off the field, securing sponsorship for a mini-bus as well as for a trophy cabinet for the clubhouse at Central Park.

1988 saw Alun Barber back in charge and, after the side had won yet again the indoor competition during the winter months at Ebbw Vale, they gained promotion back into the first division. The highlights of their League season revolved around a pair of centuries – the first by the ever-reliable Alan Cooper who made 136* against Cwmbran as Blaina rattled up 220/2, before dismissing the home side for 50 with Darryl Davies taking 5/18. a few weeks later John Prisk also posted an unbeaten century against Abercarn, as he shared a second wicket stand with Darryl Davies who also ended undefeated on 73.

John Davies, a prolific run-scorer with BSC Ebbw Vale, added some stability to a batting order which had lacked robustness the previous summer. Lady luck was also on Blaina's side, especially in the match against Tredomen when rain looked like robbing Alun Barber's side of a morale-boosting victory. With 23 to win, rain started to fall as the umpires met and agreed to further assess the situation at the end of the next over. As the precipitation started to intensify, Alan Cooper hit every delivery in the next over for four to settle the outcome. This victory proved to be a catalyst as Blaina went on to defeat Cwmbran, Brynmawr, Ponthir, the Old Monktonians and Abercarn to rise to the top of the table. Despite losing to Dinas Powis and Llantarnam, Blaina clinched promotion on August 20th with a 107-run at Ponthir.

17
THE JOY OF SIX!

There had been plenty of talk in the 1970s about Blaina CC having a new ground as the local council discussed a plan for the town and its subsequent development in the last two decades of the twentieth century. Nothing though came out of the discussions as Blaina CC were left to improve conditions at Central Park themselves. Appointed in 1977, Alan Williams subsequently became groundsman at Central Park, carefully nurturing the turf and making the horror stories, such as the 1970 debacle for 17 against Abertillery, firmly a thing of the past.

Alan also oversaw various ground improvements, including the planting at Central Park of a row of Leylandii trees at the end of the 1982 season as the club celebrated their promotion. Their planting was also part of a local biodiversity scheme, promoted by the Borough Council, to help improve the stability of the old spoil tips. It proved to be a good shelter and windbreak, as

Central Park, and the Leylandii trees in the background

well as giving something tangible back to the community at a time of hardship and job insecurity.

The hard and dedicated work of Alan Williams saw the Blaina wicket become well regarded by cricketing officials outside the town, as with players believing it to be amongst the best in Monmouthshire, if not the best in the county, the county officials increasingly allocated a series of representative matches to Central Park. For example, in 1984 it hosted fixtures for the League XI and the Under 19s, as well as in July the match between Gwent and Glamorgan 2nd XI, as future England batsman Matthew Maynard – then an aspiring tyro on the county's books – lined up at Central Park against a Gwent XI which included the prolific Blaina batsman Alan Cooper.

Five years later, July 23rd, 1989 became a red letter date both for another Blaina batsman, and the Monmouthshire club in general, as the vastly experienced Mark Davies – who had returned as captain of the Sunday XI – smashed a series of club records, and more than proved the excellent nature of Alan Williams' prized surface. In a truly remarkable innings against Rogerstone, Davies scored 275, the highest-ever innings at Central Park, as Blaina posted a mammoth 409/8 in their 40 overs.

The Central Park square

Davies, who was batting at number five in the order, raced to his century in record-breaking fashion, reaching three figures after facing just 38 balls as he put the Rogerstone attack to the sword, smashing in all, no less than 20 sixes. The Blaina bowlers then quickly worked through the visiting attack as they ended up winning by the record margin of 297 runs. This was one of four centuries which Davies posted during the summer, making 120 against Ebbw Vale, 103 versus Brynmawr and an unbeaten 146 in the contest against Abercarn.

Clive Cooper was also in outstanding form with the bat, making an unbeaten 157 against Cardiff High School Old Boys at Central Park in the first round of the Girobank Cup. His efforts saw Blaina to a 138-run victory as well as earning him a new bat from the competition's sponsors. He continued his good form in the second round at Builth Wells, posting an unbeaten 119, besides making 115 against Beechwood, as well as 111 against Worcester Nomads in a match which also saw his brother make 119.

It may have been no coincidence that the outstanding form of the Blaina batsmen came at a time when Alan Morden, a local publican and benefactor, came up with a novel idea for sponsorship for the summer by offering a pound for every six hit. After Clive Cooper's early season blitz, this was changed to a pint but, as balls regularly disappeared into the pond on the roadside boundary, as the likes of Mark Davies and John Prisk also unfurled a series of big hits, Alan Morden decided to write out a cheque instead.

Darryl Davies also made an unbeaten 108 against Brynmawr, whilst Barrie Davies, the 2nd XI captain and local publican, made 123 against Crumlin. Each amassed over 750 runs in the season – an aggregate which normally would have placed them near the top of the 1st XI batting averages. But, thanks to the outstanding work of Alan Williams and his assistant Bill Mead, these were dwarfed by Alan Cooper's tally of 852, Clive Cooper's 915, and Mark Davies' astonishing haul of 1810 runs from his 43 innings in 1989.

On the bowling front, Darryl Davies again enjoyed a decent season, opening the bowling in tandem with Steve Thomas who had also joined the club from Brynmawr. His pace and swing proved to be a huge asset, with the newcomer taking 7/39 and a hat-trick against Machen, in adddition to a return of 5/16 in a superb fifteen-over spell against Ponynewynydd.

Despite these fine individual performances, and Mark Davies' record-breaking batting, Blaina only ended up in fourth place in the league table. However, some silverware did make its way into the club's trophy cabinet, as over the winter months they won the Blaenau-Gwent Indoor cup for the fifth successive year. They also lifted the Gwent League 20-over knock-out cup, and were runners-up in the Midweek competition. Through Allen Hancock's efforts, Blaina also purchased a mini-bus for away trips as the club ended a golden decade in a very healthy state.

Over the winter months they maintained their excellent form in the indoor league at Ebbw Vale, winning the competition under the captaincy of Roy Mogford for the sixth successive time. However, when the outdoor season began, the 1st XI, now under the leadership of Mark Davies, slipped to five consecutive defeats in the league, and they did not secure a victory until June 9th when Machen were beaten. The following week, the captain struck a fine 98* as Pontnewynydd were beaten, with the victory lifting Blaina off the bottom of the table.

The following day, the game of the season took place as Blaina met Pontypridd in the second round of the Girobank Welsh Cup. This plum tie had been the reward for an earlier ten-wicket victory over Tonyrefail and, thanks to a swashbuckling 76 by David Cobourne, Blaina were able to set Pontypridd a tricky target. Their bowlers rose to the occasion as wickets fell at regular intervals, before a late rally by the Pontypridd men saw the game enter the final ball with the Taff Valley club needing four to win, and Blaina needing one wicket. All of their fielders were scattered to all points of the

Blaina CC 1st XI 1990: Back row – Tony Bye, Allen Hancock, Julian Hewitt, Alan Cooper, Darryl Davies, Alun Lewis, Alan Williams. Front Row – Mark Wilkins, Roy Mogford, Mark Davies, Alun Barber and Mark Williams

boundary as left-arm seamer Ralph Edmunds bowled the last delivery, but the batsman got a thick outside edge which saw the ball fly high over the head of wicket-keeper Alan Williams and away to the third man boundary, just out of the grasp of the fielder.

Alan Williams

Alan Williams is another stalwart of the Blaina club, having played for the 1st XI for four decades. In 1989 he featured in a record-breaking first-wicket stand, adding 196 with Alan Cooper against Monmouth, who at the time were League champions and were experimenting with a Dukes ball.

However, Monmouth's experienced bowlers found very little assistance from the new ball, and they only got a breakthrough when their fielder at deep square-leg held onto a superb catch as Cooper tried to bring up the double-century stand in the grand manner. Alan Williams then reached three figures shortly afterwards but, as he recalled in an interview for the *Taking the Field Project*, "I was a little fortunate as I had actually missed the ball attempting a leg glance, and thought the umpire would signal leg-byes. But he had failed to spot that the ball had bounced off my pads, and with no sign of a signal, I was able to raise my bat in the direction of the pavilion and celebrate the hundred."

Alan Williams (left)

Blaina duly secured a victory which helped to ease their relegation worries, and the position further improved in the final fortnight of the season, as the club clinched back-to-back victories. Thanks to another century from Alan Cooper – his sixth of the summer, equalling Mike Amos' record set back in the 1950s – plus a haul of 6/27 by Darryl Davies.

The following summer Mark Davies produced the innings of the year as he made a magnificent 192 in the Sunday friendly in mid-May against the Worcester Taverners at Central Park. Later in August, Davies made another fine hundred on home soil, as his well-crafted 128 saw the Sunday XI to victory over Newport. The Cooper brothers were also in decent form with the bat, with Alan making 98 in the away victory to Caerleon and 76 in the defeat at St.Fagans, whilst Clive made 77 in the home win over Abercynon. 1991 also saw Darryl Davies post half-centuries against Pontnewynydd and Llanwern, whilst Wayne Nash, who in July had made 145 against Blaina for RTB Ebbw Vale, made a guest appearance the following month for Blaina at Barry and scored a match-winning 68.

Blaina CC 1st XI 1991: Back row – David Evans, Alan Cooper, Darryl Davies, Spencer Matthews, Stuart Tandy, David Regan. Front Row - Clive Cooper, David Cobourne, Mark Davies, Graham Savage and Andrew Palmer

During these years, the Blaina 2nd XI also enjoyed much success, thanks in no small measure to the efforts of the likes of John Anstee and Ivor Morgan. John, or Poppy as he was affectionately known, was well-known locally for his rugby connections, but he was also a more than useful top-order batsman and shared a productive opening partnership with Barrie Davies. Ivor was a capable wicket-keeper, with the Cambridge-educated man being a handy lower order batsman. He was also Head of Physics at Aberdare Boys School, and like the other schoolmasters in the Blaina club, he took great delight in seeing the next generation of Blaina cricketers steadily emerge in the Seconds.

Memorable Matches by Darryl Davies

Number 5 – Blaina v Girlings Cwmbran at Abergavenny, August 9th, 1990

1990 was the first and only occasion when Blaina won the Gwent League 20-over knock-out cup: a competition in which they have regularly competed. Blaina reached the final of the competition after beating Old Monktonians, the Cardiff-based club, in the semi-final thanks to an astonishing blitz in the final over by Mark Davies, one of the biggest and cleanest strikers of a cricket ball in Blaina's history. After a dot ball, Mark duly struck the second ball for four, and then despatched the next four all for six as Blaina reached what became a match-winning total.

Their prize was a place in the final at the picturesque Avenue Road ground in Abergavenny against Girlings who had defeated the favourites Pontnewynydd, leaving Blaina to realise that they should not take anything for granted in the final. It proved to be a beautiful sunny evening when Blaina opted to bat first on a pristine-looking surface adjacent to the strip on which a fortnight before Glamorgan had played Worcestershire in a high-scoring draw.

Alan Cooper duly posted a memorable 101 not out as Blaina rattled up 178–3 in their allocation, with the opener receiving useful support from David Cobourne and brother Clive Cooper. At the halfway stage, Girlings were on 49–3, having been pegged back by the accurate Blaina new ball bowlers, but their middle and lower order then threw caution to the wind and, with nothing to lose, they unfurled some big shots with Ian Smith leading their rally.

Alun Barber, Blaina's evergreen seamer, then took some vital wickets to halt the counter-offensive. Aided by Allen Hancock and some good catches by Clive Cooper, Blaina won the game by forty runs with the Harding Evans Gwent League Cup being presented to captain Mark Davies by John Roberts, the chairman of the Abergavenny club.

Blaina team: Alan Cooper, David Cobourne, Mark Davies, Clive Cooper, Mark Williams, Lyndon Gore, Darryl Davies, Alun Barber, Alan Williams (wkt), Allen Hancock and Ralph Edmunds. 12th man – David Regan.

18
PROMOTION AND RELEGATION

1992 saw a re-organisation of the league structure in south-east Wales with the creation of the Glamorgan and Gwent Conference as the Gwent League merged with the Welsh Cricket conference. It created a far tougher series of fixtures for Blaina who initially played in Division Three of the new competition. After the heady years of the 1980s, hopes were high of further success, but such golden generations only come along occasionally and with the impacts of de-industrialisation making further inroads into the local economy, the club met with less success overall than in the previous decade.

There were still some of the old guard who were to the fore in the early 1990s. David Evans posted 52 and returned figures of 3/33 in the victory over Llanwern, but it was Mark Davies who led the way for the senior citizens in the side, as the batsman enjoyed fine summers in 1992 and 1993, starting with a match-winning 82 at Monmouth, and then followed by scores of 90 against Pentyrch, 82 at Cefn Forest, 73 in the home win against Beaufort, 55 against Cross Keys and 52 in the victory over Abertillery. He continued his good form in 1993, making centuries in the home wins over Barry West End and Shachelford, as well as 77 in the away win at Maesycymmer. Davies had also been one of four Blaina men to be selected for the Gwent League XI, with Davies plus the Cooper brothers and Darryl Davies all appearing against Flintshire at Brymbo in 1991.

Alan Cooper was another experienced batsman to enjoy a purple patch in 1993, scoring a match-winning 106 at Abercarn, 88 in the victory at BSC Ebbw Vale, 91 in the win at Pontnewynydd and a fine 67 in the victory against St. Fagans. The following summer, Cooper made a brilliant, and undefeated, 199 against RTB Ebbw Vale – the highest individual score in Division Three of the new League – as Blaina amassed a competition-best total of 334/4.

Darryl Davies also made some useful contributions with bat and ball, with his metronomically accurate seamers still proving to be a handful for opposing batsmen. His excellent returns included a haul of 5/35 in the victory over RTB Ebbw Vale. His lusty batting was also to the fore in the 20-overs League cup competition, although his stirring blows in the 1991 final at Abergavenny could not see Blaina to victory as Pentyrch won in the penultimate over.

Fellow veteran David Cobourne also starred in the victory at home over Llandaff in 1992, making 82 against the Cardiff-based club.

Some of the new young guns made telling contributions during the early 1990s including left-arm spinner Mark Williams who claimed 6/54 in the win in 1992 over Whitchurch-Heath to revive the glory days of left-arm twirlers at Central Park, including Vaughan Chaffey, Tommy Lloyd and Mel Gore. Andrew Palmer also recorded a couple of five-wicket hauls in 1992, taking 5/54 in the victory over Monkswood and 5/34 in defeat of Llandaff at Central Park, whilst Andrew Cecil also caught the eye with his seam bowling.

1992 also witnessed the emergence of Julian Hewitt in the Blaina batting, with the assertive left-hander posting scores of 88 in the win at Abercynon, as well as 76 in the defeat at St. Fagans. The following summer, the Yorkshire-born batsman, who had been educated at Oxford University, drew on his previous experience of playing in a good standard of cricket by making 116 in the win at Mountain Ash, as well as 81 against BSC Ebbw Vale and 77 in the match with the Tredegar Cavaliers.

Hewitt's emergence in 1992 helped to compensate for the temporary loss of the Cooper brothers, as Alan briefly switched to Ebbw Vale, and Clive joined Abertillery. Alan though was back at Blaina for 1994 as the club's decent blend of youth and experience was rewarded with silverware in 1994, firstly in the Blaenau-Gwent Midweek League where Alan Cooper starred in the semi-final victory over Ebbw Vale with a quick-fire fifty. Andrew Cecil then took 4/16 and veteran Roy Mogford 4/19 including a hat-trick as Blaina eased to a 29-run victory. This gave Alun Barber's side a place in the final against Willowtown, with the contest proving to be a dramatic affair as the match went down to the final ball.

Such an outcome seemed unlikely as Blaina made a poor start, losing Alan Cooper and Julian Hewitt with just nine runs on the board. However, a feisty innings by Lyndon Gore, who struck a pair of massive sixes got Blaina back into the game and, with David Regan hitting a couple of late boundaries, Blaina ended on 102/8. They proved to be vital runs as Willowtown mounted a run-chase with Mark Davies and Steve Williams sharing a decent stand. Their efforts meant that just 27 were needed from the last six overs, but Roy Mogford produced another inspired spell, taking 4/18 to completely change the complexion of the game. Wickets continued to tumble in the closing overs before Willowtown's last pair brought the scores level with one ball remaining. To the delight of the Blaina side, Jeff Davies was then run out off the final ball with Blaina winning the competition by virtue of losing fewer wickets.

This nail-biting win boosted morale in the Blaina ranks as, during August, they mounted a promotion bid after a series of decent victories in the Glamorgan and Gwent Conference. They clinched a place in Division Two

PROMOTION AND RELEGATION

with a six-wicket victory over Wenvoe to complete the double over the Vale of Glamorgan side which back in June had been comprehensively defeated at Central Park thanks to 127 by Alan Cooper and 102 from Julian Hewitt. Back on home soil, the Wenvoe batsmen seemed well set at 94/1, but they then alarmingly collapsed as Andrew Cecil tore through their batting line-up, taking 5/25 including a hat-trick, as he hit the stumps with three consecutive deliveries. Allen Hancock also claimed 3/30 as Wenvoe ended on just 136. Julian Hewitt then anchored the run-chase with 55, whilst Kristian Hapgood – another batsman to emerge with credit from the 2nd XI ranks in previous summers – made a solid 30, and it was fitting that Andrew Cecil was at the crease as the winning runs were made to clinch promotion.

With two games remaining, the Division Three title was still up for grabs and Blaina's next opponents were leaders Dinas Powis. Their bowling however held no terrors for Alan Cooper who made a masterly 114*, whilst Kristian Hapgood made an unbeaten 86, with the efforts of the old sorcerer and his young apprentice seeing Blaina to a decent total. After a typically

The Blaina side that were League champions in 1994. Back row – Graham Savage, Darryl Davies, Andrew Cecil, Alan Williams, Alun Lewis, Allen Hancock, Julian Hewitt, Carl Cecil. Front row – Paul Brookes, Lyn Gore, Alan Cooper, Keiron Dash, Kristian Hapgood. Inset – Alun Barber

frugal opening salvo from Darryl Davies, Julian Hewitt and Andrew Cecil worked their way through the Dinas Powis batting as Blaina won by 26 runs.

In early September Blaina secured top spot by beating Machen by eight wickets. Alan Cooper showed that he had lost none of his guile with the ball as he took 4/31, whilst Darryl Davies, Andrew Cecil and Julian Hewitt all claimed a couple of scalps each as Machen were dismissed for just 92. Cooper and Hewitt then shared a half-century stand as Blaina clinched the Division Three title with their eighth successive victory in a summer which had only seen them lose twice, with another match earlier in the year being rained off.

1995 therefore saw Blaina back in Division Two of the Conference, and Julian Hewitt celebrated their promotion in grand style in the opening match of the season, making 117 in their comprehensive victory over St. Fagans at Central Park. Shortly afterwards, John Davies nearly emulated his efforts in the home victory over Coychurch, but deprived of the strike for the final two overs, he ended unbeaten on 99. Davies was a fine left-arm seamer and a forthright batsman who had been a major force with Crumlin, and later in the season against Dinas Powis he displayed his batting talents again, but his innings of 85 was in a losing cause as Blaina faltered after their decent start, and even Roger Harvey's career-best haul of 9/28 could not clinch a victory

Back-to-back victories then followed against Blackwood and St.Fagans, with the latter game seeing Alan Cooper, who had taken over the leadership, playing a fine captain's innings with a match-winning 82, whilst in the former game, Keiron Dash made a fine 65. The following weekend, Cooper made 120 against Hoovers but his sterling efforts could not see Blaina to victory as they lost six successive games to slide again back down the table, despite another century from the veteran batsman with Cooper making 103 in the defeat against Abertillery at Central Park. This run of reversals raised the spectre of relegation, but these worries were allayed as Darryl Davies claimed 5/47 in a probing spell at Blackwood which paved the way for a badly needed win and safety in Division Two.

However, it was only a brief respite as 1996 saw Blaina lose their fight to remain in Division Two during what proved to be a disappointing summer as Alun Barber returned as captain. Despite not being in charge any more, Alan Cooper was in fine form again, twice top-scoring in tied games with Ponthir, making 80 in May and then 79 at home in July. The veteran also made 135 in the home win against Blackwood, as well as 66 in the defeat of Dinas Powis at Central Park, besides innings of 75 and 89 in the home and away losses against Abercynon. Roger Harvey had joined the club from Brynmawr and he duly took the headlines with the ball in 1996, returning figures of 6/22 in the win at Blackwood, 6/32 against Cefn Fforest and 5/35 against Ponthir. But,

PROMOTION AND RELEGATION

The Blaina 2nd XI who were League runners-up in 1994. Back row – Ivor Morgan, Redvers Price, Glen Harris, Andrew J. Williams, Stuart Hurle, Roger Harvey, Roy Mogford. Front row – Andrew Palmer, John Anstee, David Regan, Barry Davies and Graham Hughes

despite his efforts and those of Alan Cooper, Blaina found life hard in Division Two, with Alun Barber's side failing to win a game after June 8th and steadily sliding down the table as they lost ten out of eleven games in the second half of what was a modest summer for the Blaina side.

To compound matters, several players opted to retire and, with others unavailable or leaving the area, Blaina had to cancel 2nd XI fixtures as well as staging some 1st XI games with only ten men. Sadly, these trends continued to plague the club in the 1990s – a period when the club was held together by a small band of faithfuls including Alun Lewis, Alan Williams, Wayne Savage, plus brothers Andrew and Ken Palmer. Indeed, no history of the Blaina club could be written without reference to the latter's contribution with both the 1st and 2nd XI over a quarter of a century. At many times during this period, Blaina teams have been very grateful for his nagging bowling and hard-hitting

THE HISTORY OF BLAINA CRICKET CLUB

batting, whilst his shrewd analysis of the game saw him become captain of the 2nd XI in the mid 2000s, before taking over the 1st XI captaincy in 2006.

The 2nd XI were also very grateful to be able to call upon Martin Witherall, another Blaina stalwart, who showed in the late 1990s to be a very capable leader of the 2nd XI. However, there were some who felt, at a time when the club's finances remained shaky, that the Seconds were an expensive luxury and in 1997 an Extraordinary General Meeting was held at which it was discussed whether the club should only attempt to field one XI, and drop into the Alliance League along with other single XI clubs. The motion though was beaten – a decision that was to reap massive rewards in the 2000s, as the Blaina club opted to continue to raise both a 1st and 2nd XI.

In contrast to Blaina's dwindling fortunes, other sides in the area were enjoying more success and were playing in a better grade of cricket. Long-standing local rivals Abertillery had enjoyed success in the higher echelons of the Glamorgan and Gwent Conference and, in 1995, were losing finalists in the conference knock-out Cup. Ebbw Vale were also successfully competing

The Blaina CC side that won the Midweek League in 1995. Back row – Kenny Palmer, Roger Harvey, Roy Mogford, Andrew Cecil, Kristian Hapgood. Inset – Wayne Savage. Front row – Chris Regan, David Regan, Alan Cooper, Keiron Dash and Paul Brookes

in the top division of the Day's Medical Welsh Counties Cricket Alliance, besides reaching the final stages of the Welsh intermediate cup in 1995 and hosting one-day matches for Glamorgan in the Sunday League.

Abergavenny and Panteg were also successfully participating in the Crown Buckley Welsh Cricket championship against the likes of Newport, Cardiff and Swansea, whilst Indian Test cricketer Ashish Kapoor made a record score of 300 for Abergavenny against Swansea. Panteg were also able to employ overseas professionals, with Australian all-rounder Peter Underwood taking 10/61 against Bridgend Town.

For Blaina, it was case of relying on home-grown talent, with Darryl Davies returning to lead the side in 1997 as they looked to restore their fortunes back in Division Three. However, it was another season of reversals for the club as they once again spent the summer in a relegation battle. The summer began poorly with another series of reversals and it was not until late June that they got across the winning line. It was not, though, for without the want of trying, with the home game with Pontllanfraith being a microcosm of their efforts, as Alan Cooper posted an assured 70 to steer the home side to what seemed a decent total. But, despite a typically frugal spell from captain Davies, Pontllanfraith clinched victory off the penultimate ball.

The veteran batsman also twice made 116 on his favourite wicket at Central Park, with the first seeing Blaina to a badly needed win over Abercarn. A fortnight later he repeated the trick against Treorchy, but once again the visitors cruised to victory as Blaina remained towards the foot of the table. Indeed, their slide down the conference tables mirrored the rise in the area's unemployment as Blaenau Gwent became Wales' unemployment blackspot, with the figure for those receiving benefit in the first three months of 1997 standing at 10.4%, well above the Welsh average of 7.5%.

In previous years of high unemployment, the success of the Blaina cricket had cheered up the sporting community, but this was not the case in the closing years of the 1990s as the club took part in games in the Fourth Division.

Well Done Alan!

Alan Cooper has scored more centuries for Blaina than any other batsman, although the fact that several scorebooks are missing, means that nobody is certain precisely how many he has made during his career for the 1st XI since the late 1970s. There are records of 40 three-figure scores, so the true figure could be closer to 50 or even higher.

THE HISTORY OF BLAINA CRICKET CLUB

Alan Cooper batting in the 1980s

The opening batsman is just one of many Alan's to have played with distinction for Blaina – in fact in the late 1970s there were times when he was joined by seven others – Alan Davies, Alan Williams, Alun Lewis, Allen Hughes, Alun Barber, Alan Brookes and Alan Crook! In fact, in the match against Pentwyn on a damp early season wicket, all of the visiting batsmen were dismissed by Blaina bowlers whose Christian name was either Alan, Alun or Allen.

The fall of each wicket was duly greeted by a stentorian shout of "Well done, Alan" by Blaina's staunchest supporter Jim Taylor, and by the end of the Pentwyn innings, his words drew a few puzzled looks on the faces of the visitors who could not believe at first that every wicket-taking bowler was indeed called Alan!

To compound matters, when Blaina began their innings, Alan Williams got off the mark with a huge six, prompting another cry of "Well done, Alan" from the boundary's edge. The Pentwyn fielders then entered into the spirit of things as Alan Leighton took the first six Blaina wickets with the fall of each man being greeted by shouts of "Well done, Alan" from the field. But Jim Taylor was not going to be outdone, and the remarkable sequence of events continued as Alun Barber and Alan Brookes then saw Blaina home in a nail biting finish with the two men leaving the field to a delighted cry of "Well done Alan, Well done, Alun!"

PROMOTION AND RELEGATION

Alan Cooper receiving a hinged stump from Club Patron David Jones, on becoming a life member of Blaina Cricket Club

There was little talk of promotion as a further re-building exercise took place under Alun Barber's captaincy. Several of the old stalwarts gave way to fresh blood, but Alan Cooper, the evergreen Peter Pan of Blaina cricket, was still to the fore, making 110 in the victory in 1999 against Tredegar Southend as well as later in the year 4/46 against Owens Corning. But a desperately inexperienced 2nd XI took to the field, and it was no surprise that they went through 1999 without a single success. In his remarks at the AGM, Chairman Wayne Savage commended everyone for their wholehearted efforts and boundless enthusiasm, besides hoping that for all concerned the 2000s would see a return to more successful times. His words duly proved to be prescient.

19
BLAINA CC ENTERS THE TWENTY-FIRST CENTURY

Historians may argue about whether 2000 or 2001 marks the start of the 21st century, but one thing about which there is no dispute is that Blaina CC, after a prolonged cycle of industrial growth and decline, civic unrest and the ravages caused by unemployment, were now in the third century of their existence.

A further re-organisation of the league structure saw Blaina start 2000 in Division Two of the Welsh Club Conference, with events on the field being a portent of what was to follow for the next few summers, as Blaina tasted defeat more often than success. The evergreen Alun Barber returned to the captaincy in 2000, thereby earning the distinction of leading the 1st XI across four decades. He had as his deputy Dick Edwards, as well as being able to call upon the services of other experienced players such as Alan Cooper and Allen Hancock. Despite the reversals, some new faces did emerge, including wicket-keeper Graham Griffin who moved over from the other side of Mynydd Garn–y-Cefn following the disbanding of the BSC Ebbw Vale club with whom Blaina had enjoyed a good relationship.

Wayne Savage succeeded Barber in 2001 and, for a few weeks in the opening part of the season, it looked as if the new skipper might enjoy more success on the field than his predecessor had done. The summer began with a three-wicket win over Wenvoe, thanks to a half-century by Gavin Griffiths and a steady knock by Darryl Davies, as Blaina reached their target in near darkness. The following week Dick Edwards helped to bowled Blaina to another victory as he returned figures of 3/10 from 15 frugal overs against Monkswood.

A five-wicket win then followed over Pentwyn to raise hopes of a hugely successful summer, but this decent start had masked a lack of strength in depth as a string of defeats then followed, whilst the Blaina club were also docked points for failing to raise a 2nd XI for various fixtures. Many youngsters, who in previous years had been the mainstay of the 2nd XI, had other sporting interests, whilst the cost of teas plus a match fee was quite a sizeable outlay for someone who was not guaranteed work. Rob Smith, who captained the 2nd XI in 2002, did a magnificent job during this time in keeping

BLAINA CC ENTERS THE TWENTY-FIRST CENTURY

the team together, besides leading by example with a tremendous spell of 4/22 in fifteen overs helping to secure victory over Pontllanfraith.

Despite these experiences, Wayne Savage continued as captain of the 1st XI in 2002 but, despite Savage's forthright batting, it was another summer when victories were few and far between. He duly handed over the baton to Dick Edwards in 2003, but once again, Blaina remained in the lower part of the table as they failed to string together a series of victories. Some of the youngsters, who had been thrown in at the deep end in the previous years, started to make headway, with Lee Davies and Mark Evans emerging as decent players. The former struck 75 against Great Western, as well as another fine half-century in the 68-run victory over Monkswood. Evans also recorded three fifties himself, but overall there was still an over-reliance on Wayne Savage's batting, as well as the clever captaincy of Dick Edwards whose subtle tactics dug the side out of a hole on more than one occasion.

But any small shoots of recovery that may have started to sprout in 2003 had disappeared within twelve months as, under Alun Barber's captaincy, Blaina enjoyed a further summer of disappointment and defeat in 2004. Their batting was stronger as a result of the recruitment of Daniel Edwards from Abertillery, but only two victories were recorded all summer, and no less than thirty players took to the field for the 1st XI. No settled side emerged and each week a different eleven was chosen, highlighting the lack of consistency as well as the absence of a talented nucleus, as had been the case a few years before.

The situation marginally improved in 2005, but there was still great reliance on Daniel Edwards and Wayne Savage. The one promising sign in the 1st XI was that Gavin Griffiths showed promise as a top order batsman with a fine 128 against Crumlin, as well as scores of 63 and 68 in the games against Penarth. Andrew Rowson also gave some displays of explosive hitting, including 72 against St. Peter's at Central Park, but the most important innings as far as the recent history of the Blaina club has been concerned came in the Past v Present match as Chris Despres made 57 and, after play, discussing the possibility of returning to Blaina to help out his old club. He duly returned for the next couple of weekends and, after being particularly impressed by the talented young players in the youth section, he agreed to assist with the coaching of the next generation of Blaina cricketers as well as leading the 2nd XI where the youngsters were being blooded.

During his coaching stints in the Ebbw Vale Indoor School, Despres' eye was particularly taken by fast bowler Adam Lane, batsman–offspinner Daniel Wall, wicket-keeper batsman Liam Crandon, batsmen Josh Samuel and Nathan Cobourne, swing bowler Jack Singh and spinner Andrew Langridge.

THE HISTORY OF BLAINA CRICKET CLUB

The participants in the Past and Present match in 2007. Back row – Darryl Davies, Wayne Savage, Andrew Langridge, Andrew Rowson, Daniel Edwards, Andrew J. Williams, Nick Williams, Gavin Griffiths, Matthew Kedward, Adam Lane, Kenny Palmer. Front Row – David Cobourne, David Morgan, Cole Rogers, Daniel Wall, Liam Crandon, Keiron Meek, Jack Singh, Josh Samuel, Matthew Bull. Holding stump at front is Andrew Palmer.

Together with David Edwards and brothers Jack and Rhys Savage, these young cricketers formed the nucleus of the 2nd XI in the course of the next few seasons, as well as making occasional appearances for the 1st or Sunday elevens to further their experience.

Evidence of the rising morale in the club came in the opening fixture of the 2006 season as Gavin Griffiths began in grand style with 109 against Monkswood. Wicket-keeper Daniel Edwards also got his name on the centurions board with 104 against St.Peter's, whilst Grant Gwillym posted 78 against Pontnewynedd and 55 in the game with Bridgend. However, the highlight of the 2006 season was undoubtedly the opening stand of 200 recorded by Wayne Savage (119) and Gavin Griffiths (91) against Crumlin.

The green shoots of recovery were starting to sprout and, during the winter months, the club had further boosts as, firstly, experienced seam bowler Clayton Lane, now living in Port Talbot, agreed to travel to Blaina to take charge of 1st XI affairs. There was further good news as Alan Cooper agreed to come out of retirement and to play again in 2007, whilst his brother Clive also agreed to turn out whenever his work commitments permitted. It did not take either of them very long to get back in the runs, with Clive making 109 on his return to action against Sully 3rd XI, whilst Alan made 119 at Penarth in his second innings back in the 1st XI. The presence of the two vastly experienced players was a massive boost, whilst they both proved to be superb role models for the pool of youngsters being groomed under Chris Despres' tutelage.

2008 was another year of steady consolidation for the 1st XI, with Alan Cooper adding further to his remarkable tally of centuries, making 145 against Mountain Ash and 132 in the game with Whitchurch-Heath. Daniel Edwards also struck 101 in the match with Croesyceiliog, whilst several of the youngsters in the 2nd XI gained further invaluable experience in the senior side with fourteen year-old Daniel Wall coming close to becoming the club's youngest ever centurion with 83 for the Sunday XI against Tredegar.

On the bowling front, captain Alun Barber produced the standout performances, with hauls of 4/7 against Sully, 4/12 against Whitchurch-Heath and 4/34 in the match against Lisvane. He was duly re-appointed as captain for 2009 – his fourteenth year in charge breaking the great Evan Watkins' record of thirteen. Andrew Palmer, another stalwart of the club, reached a personal milestone in 2009 as in early May he posted his maiden century. Back in 2007, he had been awarded Life Membership of the club, and in his acceptance speech, Andrew said that the only thing he had failed to do during his time at the club was to score a century. With his tongue firmly in his cheek, he said that he thought that various captains had missed a trick by asking him to bat as low as number ten. But he proved that he was up to the job, especially after many long hours of practice against the bowling machine at the Ebbw Vale Indoor School, as he made 104 against Brynmawr.

Other veterans continued to put in decent performances with Clive Cooper getting the 2009 season off to a great start with 111 at Croesyceiliog, whilst Darryl Davies made 86 against Chepstow. But the greatest achievements overall were the 2nd XI securing promotion and the continued blossoming of the youngsters in Chris Despres' care. Fifteen year-old Josh Samuel made 108 against Penydarren at Central Park, with his innings showing great maturity and wise shot selection, whilst Liam Crandon also came within one run of his maiden hundred with 99 against Porth.

Andrew Palmer

The Mel Morris Trophy

Mel Morris was a stalwart of the Blaina club. He started playing in 1948 and for the next thirty years he gave fine service to the Club. During the 1950s, Mel struck up a fine bowling partnership with left-arm quick bowler Mostyn Williams, before leading the club in 1957, and again in 1965 and 1967. The latter two were difficult times for the Club, but he guided them through the choppy waters.

His reward for outstanding service was the presentation of Life Membership in 1980, and the inauguration of the Mel Morris Trophy for the Clubman of the Year – the most coveted award given annually at the Club's Dinner.

The progress of these young colts greatly thrilled the older members of the squad who, unlike some in other clubs, showed no envy or animosity against the rising stars. Indeed, Alan Cooper drew attention to their emergence in the 1st XI during his acceptance speech after also being made a Life Member of the club. It was no surprise therefore that at the end of the summer, Chris Despres was invited to lead the 1st XI in 2010. He had been the skipper back in 1980 so after a gap of thirty years, it gave him immense pleasure to lead the side into the field again, especially as it included so many of the youngsters whose progress he had overseen.

He also became the club's second oldest captain behind Evan Watkins, whilst on a personal level he was delighted that on several occasions his two sons Gareth and Jo were chosen for the 1st XI. Both had been no more than toddlers when their father had last led the club, and three decades later, their experience of club cricket in the Bristol area helped to strengthen the Blaina batting. This was especially important as a restructuring of the League had taken place over the winter months, and 2010 saw Blaina playing one division higher than in previous years. Given their form in the course of the

The participants in the Dads and Sons match at Tintern in 2009. Back row – Kenny Palmer, Keith Edwards, Terry Wall, Paul Lane, John Crandon, Malcolm Samuel, Andrew Langridge, David Cobourne. Front row – Cole Rogers, David Edwards, Daniel Wall, Adam Lane, Liam Crandon, Josh Samuel, Jack Singh and Nathan Cobourne

previous decade, some felt that 2010 would therefore be a difficult summer for Chris Despres' team, but the 1st XI duly produced some of their best cricket for many years.

Joe Despres set the tone in the opening games with 81 against Bridgend Town, followed by 69 versus Crumlin, before Darryl Davies weighed in with scores of 96 against Brynmawr, 70 against Barry Wanderers at Central Park and 64 in the contest with Penarth as Blaina completed a sequence of six successive victories. Their winning run was also helped by two further centuries from the evergreen Alan Cooper who made 154 in the victory over Monkswood and 138 in the win against Lisvane, thereby completing the outstanding achievement of scoring centuries in five different decades.

His fine efforts saw Blaina into second place in the table: a position they maintained into July and August, with Adam Lane taking 6/37 against Pontllanfraith, whilst Justin Watts – a fast bowler recruited from Ebbw Vale – meant that Blaina's new ball attack had a potent cutting edge for the first time in several seasons. The combined efforts of the batsmen and bowlers meant

Blaina CC 1st XI 2010: Back row – Adam Lane, Michael Clarke, Jack Singh, Gareth Pagett, Liam Crandon, Alan Cooper. Front Row – Alun Barber, Joe Despres, Chris Despres, Gareth Despres and Daniel Wall

that Blaina remained in the promotion hunt with the season culminating in a head-to-head on August 28th away to leaders Barry Wanderers. It was a game which Blaina needed to win in order to secure promotion, but the home side's bowling proved too strong as the Barry team won by seven wickets.

This defeat, plus results elsewhere meant that Blaina ended up in third place, but nobody associated with the club was that disappointed as during the year, the youngsters had blossomed at 1st XI level, as epitomised by two fine innings from Liam Crandon. The pupil at Clifton College made 80 against Blaengarw, before making a magnificent 172 for the Sunday XI against Tredegar, displaying a wide array of sweetly-timed shots all around the wicket, as the youngster expertly dissected the field.

20
BLAINA CRICKET CLUB IN 2011

Nearly 160 years after the first record of cricket in the Monmouthshire town, Blaina CC started the 2011 season full of optimism for the future. Their upbeat mood and great hope for the youth of the club was evident in the decision to appoint Adam Lane as captain with the youngster, at 21, becoming the club's youngest-ever captain. After an excellent attendance at winter and pre-season nets, this feelgood factor was maintained as the season began with victories in the friendlies against Pontllanfraith and Llanarth, with the latter match seeing Gareth Pagett take a hat-trick. Despite his work commitments over a number of years, Gareth has shown an ability to turn a game on its head, and his bowling, allied to his safe fielding, could see him become a major figure in the coming years.

A modern day Blaina CC cap

BLAINA CRICKET CLUB IN 2011

After a couple of defeats in the opening League games, the first victory in the competition duly came at Shirenewton as Chepstow 3rd XI were beaten by seven wickets as Ross Watts posted an unbeaten 106, Gareth Despres made 81 and Jack Singh claimed his first five-wicket haul for the 1st XI. Daniel Wall then posted a match-winning 92 against Pontllanfraith, whilst Alun Morgan – another recruit from Ebbw Vale – set up victory over Penarth with a fine half-century as Adam Lane and Jack Singh scrambled the winning runs off the penultimate ball of the contest. The innings of the summer came from Ross Watts who made a chanceless and unbeaten 142 against Radyr. But rain dampened any aspirations of promotion for both the 1st and 2nd elevens, with the latter again boasting some rich talent for the future including all-rounder James Selway whose fielding ranks amongst the best-ever seen at Central Park.

2011 also saw Michael Clarke continue his progress as a talented batsman, whilst Chris Sutton also enjoyed a successful first summer with Blaina. Chris, who has played for Sussex Colts, made some telling contributions during the course of the summer with his off-spin, none more so than in the final game of the summer when he secured 3/33 off his allotted overs, before making an unbeaten 39 to allow Blaina to amass sufficient batting points to secure their position for the 2012 season.

Ken Cayford – Blaina's Only Dual Life Member

The end of season awards night in 1980 saw Ken Cayford become a Life Member of the town's cricket club. He therefore achieved the distinction of being the only person to have been appointed a Life Member of both Blaina RFC and Blaina CC. He had first played for the town's cricket club in 1958 and even after retiring, he was a constant figure behind the scenes, whether it being scoring, umpiring or generally supporting the club.

Blaina CC is therefore in rude health as it heads towards its second century, and all despite no major sponsor and the complete disintegration of the heavy industry which had been the bulwark of the club in the 19th and early 20th century. The post-industrial landscape in the Monmouthshire valleys is very different to the one enjoyed by the ironmasters and colliery owners when coal was king. The fact that the club has successfully ridden out the slumps in the local and national economy is testament to the fortitude of the club's great servants, celebrated in the preceding chapters, as well as to the strong and indelible links with the local community which has nursed the town's cricket club through thick and thin.

THE HISTORY OF BLAINA CRICKET CLUB

The 1988 Bed Push featuring (left to right) Kenny Palmer, Chris Regan, Brian Sillman, Redvers Price, Andrew Palmer, John Prisk, Tim Furber, Andrew J. Williams and Alan Williams

A presentation of a signed bat to Mayor Peter Law in 1989, including David Regan, John Wright, Alan Morden, Wayne Savage, Redvers Price, Chris Regan, Alun Lewis, John Prisk, Ralph Edmunds, Andrew J. Williams, Alan Cooper, Clive Cooper, Stuart Hurle, Barrie Davies, Roy Mogford, Keiron Dash and Kenny Palmer. In the front row are Brian Sillman, Alan Williams, Peter Law and Andrew Palmer

BLAINA CRICKET CLUB IN 2011

This symbiotic relationship with the local community has been clearly in evidence in the past three decades as Blaina CC have undertaken some ingenious forms of fund-raising. These novel efforts began in 1982 when club member David Morgan undertook a sponsored parachute jump and was followed in 1988 with a sponsored bed-push over fourteen miles from Blaina to Nevill Hall Hospital in Abergavenny. In recent years there have been other sponsored walks and a diverse range of activities including jumble sales, quizzes, car boot sales plus the sale of tickets under a reciprocal arrangement with Carmarthen Town AFC. Proceeds for the club have also been raised from the club's sale of cans of beer and lager after play, especially now that the Old Hafodians club has closed leaving the town bereft of the traditional location where over the years, scores of Blaina cricketers and other sportsmen gathered to either celebrate victory or drown their sorrows after defeat. All of these activities have helped to swell the club's coffers at a time when their officials have had to keep membership fees at a very low level of £2, ever mindful of the fact that so many people in the local area are either out of work or are in part-time employment.

Over the years, the club has also benefitted from its strong, family atmosphere. For example, during the 1980s David Regan and his two nephews Chris and Barrie, frequently played alongside each other, either for the 1st or the 2nd XI. David – or "Cousin Logie" as he was known after the diminutive West Indian batsman Gus Logie, was also a capable captain, successfully leading the 2nd XI in 1992. In recent seasons, the presence of three brothers in various Blaina line-ups has been maintained by triplets Nick, Miles and Tom Williams. All three have played with distinction at 1st and 2nd XI level since they joined the club in the late 1990s – Tom is a lively fast bowler, Miles is a combative wicket-keeper batsman, whilst Nick is a handy swing bowler who captained the 2nd XI in 2010 and played a big part in the side gaining promotion the season before.

The survival of Blaina CC and the continuation of a vibrant, enthusiastic and forward-thinking attitude is also the result of the actions of a core group of people best epitomised by the likes of Alan and Diane Williams who have freely given countless hours of their time to the club's affairs, and all in return for the safe and happy knowledge that everything is well with events at Central Park. Alan first played for Blaina in 1960, and over fifty years later he still takes great pride in the excellence of the surface which he has helped to create. Diane has cheerfully made countless teas for the club's players and supporters, besides helping Alan make the captain's board which adorns the Blaina pavilion, and wholeheartedly and enthusiastically throwing herself into researching the club's history and gathering the information on which this book is based. Her sterling efforts are even more remarkable given the fact that she does not actually like watching cricket herself, and originally became involved with Blaina CC in the 1970s when player's wives decided to start making teas in order to help raise money for the cash-strapped club.

Alun Lewis is another man to have given lifelong service to the club. Having played his first game in 1964, he joined the committee three years later, before becoming Treasurer in 1969 and then Secretary from 1973. He has even dipped into his own pocket to help keep Blaina CC afloat, besides fending off advances from Blaina RFC for extending the rugby pitches onto the cricket field and Alan Williams' hallowed turf.

It is because of the wholehearted efforts of the likes of people such as Alan and Diane Williams, plus Alun Lewis, Andrew and Ken Palmer, plus all of the other volunteers that Blaina Cricket Club has survived. It is precisely the reason as well that the club – founded by the ironmasters who have long since departed from the winding valleys of Monmouthshire – should be poised to proudly celebrate a second centenary in the coming years as South Wales further develops its post-industrial and service-based economy. Tales about the deeds of the current crop of rising stars such as Liam Crandon, have yet to occur, but in the fullness of time, they too will deserve to be added to the history chronicled in the previous chapters, and the remarkable efforts of the likes of Evan Watkins, TT Williams and the Cooper brothers. Yes, it's a little club, but as I'm sure you will now appreciate, they have certainly enjoyed a big story.

Central Park in the snow

APPENDICES

A. Captains of Blaina CC: 1889–2012

1889	PERCY MARTIN
1890	PERCY MARTIN
1891	T. GABB
1892	T. GABB
1893	T. GABB
1894	T. GABB
1895	TOM L. DAVIES
1896	R. NORFOLK
1897	T. CANNON
1898	T. CANNON
1899	T. CANNON
1900	W. LLOYD
1901	TOM L. DAVIES
1902	R. JONES
1903	TOM L. DAVIES
1904	TOM L. DAVIES
1905	J.C. NEAT
1906	J.C. NEAT
1907	J.C. NEAT
1908	TOM L. DAVIES
1909	TOM L. DAVIES
1910	TOM L. DAVIES
1911	TOM L. DAVIES
1912	TOM L. DAVIES
1913	TOM L. DAVIES
1914	*Unknown*
1915–1918	**No Play**
1919	EVAN W. WATKINS
1920	EVAN W. WATKINS
1921	EVAN W. WATKINS
1922	EVAN W. WATKINS
1923	EVAN W. WATKINS
1924	EVAN W. WATKINS

N.B. There is no record of the Club's captain prior to the 1889 season

APPENDICES

1925	EVAN W. WATKINS
1926	EVAN W. WATKINS
1927	EVAN W. WATKINS
1928	EVAN W. WATKINS
1929	EVAN W. WATKINS
1930	EVAN W. WATKINS
1931	W.H. JENKINS
1932	W.H. JENKINS
1933	W.H. JENKINS
1934	J. MOODY
1935	ALBERT PROUT
1936	ALBERT PROUT
1937	ALBERT PROUT
1938	JOHN GOMERY
1939	JOHN GOMERY
1940–1945	**No Play**
1946	EVAN W. WATKINS
1947	PHIL. JAMES
1948	GOMER EVANS
1949	PHIL. JAMES
1950	WILLIAM DAVIES
1951	RUMSEY JAMES
1952	RUMSEY JAMES
1953	MOSTYN WILLIAMS
1954	RUMSEY JAMES
1955	DON JONES
1956	GRAHAM LOCKSTONE
1957	MEL. MORRIS
1958	GLYN HARVEY
1959	GOMER EVANS
1960	GOMER EVANS
1961	MEL. GORE
1962	MEL. GORE
1963	ERNIE J. FEARN
1964	DAVID POPE AND DAVID JONES
1965	MEL. MORRIS
1966	ERNIE J. FEARN
1967	MEL. MORRIS

APPENDICES

Year	Name
1968	ERNIE J. FEARN
1969	GWYN EVANS
1970	JOHN WALDING
1971	HOWARD GRIFFITHS
1972	DON. MAIDMENT
1973	DON. MAIDMENT
1974	NORMAN BIRD AND ANTHONY EDWARDS
1975	MEL. GORE
1976	ALAN DAVIES
1977	ALUN BARBER
1978	ALUN BARBER
1979	CHRIS. DESPRES
1980	CHRIS. DESPRES
1981	ALUN LEWIS
1982	ALUN LEWIS
1983	ALUN LEWIS
1984	ALUN BARBER
1985	DARRYL DAVIES
1986	STEVE. WILLIAMS
1987	ALAN WILLIAMS
1988	ALUN BARBER
1989	ALUN BARBER
1990	MARK DAVIES
1991	MARK DAVIES
1992	ALUN BARBER
1993	ALUN BARBER
1994	ALUN BARBER
1995	ALAN COOPER
1996	ALUN BARBER
1997	DARRYL DAVIES
1998	ALUN BARBER
1999	ALUN BARBER
2000	ALUN BARBER
2001	WAYNE SAVAGE
2002	WAYNE SAVAGE
2003	DICK EDWARDS
2004	ALUN BARBER
2005	GRAHAM GRIFFIN
2006	KEN PALMER

APPENDICES

2007	CLAYTON LANE
2008	CLAYTON LANE
2009	ALUN BARBER
2010	CHRIS DESPRES
2011	ADAM LANE
2012	ADAM LANE

B. First date of matches played by cricket clubs in the Blaina & Nantyglo area

1853	Blaina
1892	Garnvach
1894	Blaina United
1894	Blaina Lancaster
1894	Blaina Cemetary
1894	Nantyglo Wesleyans
1899	Blaina West End
1899	Blaina Congregational
1900	Nantyglo Holy Trinity
1902	Blaina Nondescripts
1903	Blaina Prims Methodist
1906	Winchestown
1909	Blaina Salemites
1910	Blaina Excelsiors
1910	Cwmcelyn
1910	Blaina Berea
1910	Blaina Globeites
1910	Blaina Imperials
1913	Blaina Corinthians
1914	Claytown
1914	Nantyglo Imperials
1922	Bourneville
1923	Blaina Hornets
1927	Blaina Wesleyans
1932	Duffryn United
1938	Waunmarsley
1938	Blaina Sports Club
1952	Duffryn Sports club
1966	Semtex

APPENDICES

C. Century makers for Blaina CC

MIKE AMOS	9	1960, 1961, 1962, 1963
NORMAN BAINTON	2	1932
NORMAN BIRD	1	1975
ALAN COOPER	40+	1979, 1981, 1983, 1988, 1989, 1990, 1993, 1994, 1995, 1996, 1997, 1999, 2000, 2007, 2008, 2009, 2010
CLIVE COOPER	8	1985, 1989, 2007, 2009
DAVID COBOURNE	1	1986
LIAM CRANDON	1	2010
KEIRON DASH	2	1994, 1995
ROY DASH	1	1954
BARRIE DAVIES	5	1989, 1990, 1994, 1995
DARRYL DAVIES	3	1987–1989
KENNETH DAVIES	1	1933
MARK DAVIES	10	1979, 1985, 1989, 1990, 1991, 1993
WILLIAM H. DAVIES	1	1947
CHRIS DESPRES	1	1983
DANIEL EDWARDS	2	2006, 2008
GOMER EVANS	2	1949, 1952
GARETH GILLINGHAM	2	1978
LYNDON GORE	1	1988
GAVIN GRIFFITHS	4	2004, 2005, 2006
HOWARD GRIFFITHS	1	1975
GRANT GWILYM	2	2007, 2008
CHRISTIAN HAPGOOD	1	1990
ROGER HARVEY	1	1997
JULIAN HEWITT	4	1993, 1994, 1995
RUMSEY JAMES	2	1947, 1954
BRYN JONES	1	1935
HOWARD KNIGHT	1	1960
ADAM LANE	1	2010
GARY NICKLIN	2	1976
ANDREW PALMER	1	2009
RICHARD PARRY	1	1929
H.J.POPE (JOE)	1	1928
JOHN PRISK	2	1986, 1988
JOSH SAMUEL	1	2009
WAYNE SAVAGE	1	2006

TOM TAYLOR	1	1911
EVAN W. WATKINS	3	1919, 1921, 1922
ROSS WATTS	2	2011
ALAN WILLIAMS	3	1980, 1982, 1990
DICK WILLIAMS	1	1984
MARK WILLIAMS	1	1990

D. Life Members of Blaina CC

1931	EVAN WATKINS
1932	RICHARD JOHN WETHERALL
1934	TOM LLOYD DAVIES, VAUGHAN CHAFFEY
1938	HARRY JACK HALE
1947	ALBERT PROUT
1949	HERBERT WILLIAMS, REES PRICE
1951	WILLIAM H. DAVIES
1958	JOE DALLY
1964	GOMER EVANS
1970	GEORGE LANGLEY
1975	DON MAIDMENT
1977	ERNIE FEARN, BRYN WILTSHIRE
1980	MEL. MORRIS
1981	KENNY CAYFORD
1999	ALAN WILLIAMS
2000	ALUN LEWIS
2001	ALUN BARBER
2003	REDVERS PRICE
2006	DARRYL DAVIES
2007	ANDREW PALMER
2009	ALAN COOPER

E. Chairmen of Blaina CC

1920–1921	WILLIAM H. SILK
1922–1924	HERBERT WILLIAMS
1925–1930	IVOR JONES
1931–1933	JOHN JARVIS
1934	REES PRICE
1935	IVOR JONES

1936	JOHN JARVIS
1937	IVOR JONES
1938–1948	WILLIAM H. SILK
1949	HERBERT WILLIAMS
1950	WILLIAM H. SILK
1951–1952	ALBERT CLARKE
1953–1955	WILLIAM PARHAM
1956–1957	REES PRICE
1958–1963	ALBERT CLARKE
1964–1966	RON ADAMS
1967	ALBERT CLARKE
1968	GEORGE LANGLEY
1969	ERNIE FEARNE
1970–1971	ALAN WILLIAMS
1972–1974	DON MAIDMENT
1975–1976	PAUL JAMES
1977–1983	ALAN WILLIAMS
1984–1988	BRIAN SILLMAN
1989–1991	DARRYL DAVIES
1992–1993	TONY BYE
1994	MARK DAVIES
1995–1996	REDVERS PRICE
1997–2000	WAYNE SAVAGE
2001	ROB SMITH
2002–2003	WAYNE SAVAGE
2004–2012	ANDREW PALMER

F. Secretaries of Blaina CC

1889–1890	R. NORFOLK
1891–1892	F. GUNTER
1893	*Unknown*
1894	J. OWEN
1895–1896	R. PAGE
1897	*Unknown*
1898	D. PRITCHARD
1899	*Unknown*
1900–1904	W. JONES
1905–1907	*Unknown*

APPENDICES

1908–1912	D. PRITCHARD
1913	B. JONES
1914	*Unknown*
1919–1921	D.L. JONES
1922–1933	RICHARD J.WETHERALL
1934	J. MOODY
1935–1937	JOHN H. GOMERY
1938–1951	RICHARD J. WEATHERALL
1952	FRED G. HAYTER
1953–1954	IVOR WILLIAMS
1955–1957	JIM GARROWAY
1958–1966	ERNIE FEARNE
1967	KEITH THOMAS
1968	ERNIE FEARNE
1969	ALAN WILLIAMS
1970–1972	ERNIE FEARN
1973–2012	ALUN LEWIS

G. Treasurers of Blaina CC

1889–1890	R. PEARSON
1891–1892	M. TRUE
1893	*Unknown*
1894	T. DREW
1895–1896	J.H. JONES
1897	*Unknown*
1898–1902	C.COOPER
1903–1904	B. DAVIES
1905–1907	*Unknown*
1908–1913	H. CHAMBERS
1914	*Unknown*
1919–1921	RICHARD J. WETHERALL
1922–1937	ARTHUR LOCKSTONE
1938–1939	J.WELLINGTON
1946–1955	ARTHUR LOCKSTONE
1956–1957	GLYN HARVEY
1958	MIKE AMOS
1959–1964	DON MAIDMENT
1965–1966	WILLIAM H. DAVIES

APPENDICES

1967	KEITH DASH
1968	MEL MORRIS
1969	KEITH THOMAS
1970–1972	ALUN LEWIS
1973–1974	ALAN BROOKES
1975–1978	PETER SIMS
1979	ALUN LEWIS
1980–1981	GARETH GILLINGHAM
1982–1984	DAVID MORGAN
1985–2012	ALUN LEWIS

H. Presidents of Blaina CC

1889–1892	JOHN DAKERS
1893	*Unknown*
1894	JOHN DAKERS
1895–1896	Dr. H.C. BEVAN
1897–1902	*Unknown*
1903–1911	M. WOLSTENHOLME
1912–1914	Dr. H.C. BEVAN
1919–1920	JOSEPH PARRY
1921–1927	TOM L. DAVIES
1928–1930	JOSEPH PARRY
1931–1950	EVAN SILK
1951–1952	WILLIAM H. SILK
1953–1954	EVAN SILK
1955–1972	WILLIAM H. PRITCHARD
1973–1975	ERNIE FEARN
1976–1979	DAVID WATKINS
1980–1981	GEORGE LANGLEY
1982–1983	AUSTIN WHEELER
1984–2006	PETER LAW
2007–2012	MARTIN WITHERALL

I. Patrons of Blaina CC

1951–1954	EVAN SILK
1955–1964	SELWYN PARRY

APPENDICES

1965–1972	C. WILLIAMS
1973–1984	WILLIAM H. PRITCHARD
1985–1987	ERNIE J. FEARN
1988–1990	TERRY MORGAN
1991–1994	GRAHAM COBOURNE
1995–2003	ERNIE FEARN
2004–2007	MEL MORRIS
2008–2012	DAVID JONES